West Academic Publishing's Law School Advisory Board

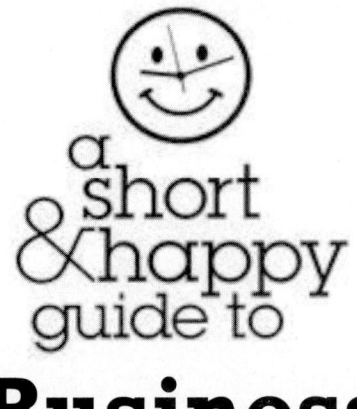

Business Contracts

Rachel J. Barnett
Lecturer in Law
Columbia Law School

A SHORT & HAPPY GUIDE® SERIES

WEST
ACADEMIC
PUBLISHING

a short & happy guide series is a trademark registered in the U.S. Patent and Trademark Office.

© 2017 LEG, Inc. d/b/a West Academic

    444 Cedar Street, Suite 700
    St. Paul, MN 55101
    1-877-888-1330

Printed in the United States of America

ISBN: 978-1-64020-072-2

Legal Disclaimer

The information in this book should not be construed as legal advice or legal opinion on specific facts. This book is not intended to be a definitive statement on the subject matter addressed. Rather, it is intended for general understanding and to provide practical tools and references. It is meant to make you smarter and improve your communications with attorneys to seek the right advice and make the contracting process more transparent and efficient. Your use of this book does not in itself establish an attorney-client relationship with the author or any contributor.

All content in this book is presented AS-IS, WITH NO WARRANTIES OF ANY NATURE, EXPRESS OR IMPLIED; USE AT YOUR OWN RISK. If you do not know what the previous sentence means, you have much to learn (for starters, check out the section on warranty disclaimers herein). Every case is unique, and laws and regulations change constantly. If you have questions or concerns about legal documents, feel free to discuss them with an attorney. Oh, and any views that might be expressed here are the author's and not necessarily those of any current or former employers, colleagues or anyone else.

Rachel J. Barnett

July 2017

Acknowledgments

I would like to thank the many people who have made this book possible.

First, to Avery Katz for giving me the opportunity to teach a course at Columbia Law School that simulates real life challenges faced by legal departments, and to Louise Firestone for taking this journey with me. I would also like to express my sincere gratitude to those that read through the book's many drafts, Alan Howard, David Glogoff, Kristin Pauley and my editor, Jill Nawrocki. Thank you for taking time out of your busy schedules to provide helpful suggestions and thoughtful feedback to move this project forward.

I would like to thank Courtney Maggart and Lily Gunn Townsend for encouraging me to do this in the first place. You convinced me to write down my thoughts to make it easier for anyone to understand complex legal concepts. Had it not been for our conversation over pizza and wine in Palm Springs, this book would not have come to fruition.

Most importantly, I would like to thank my husband Jeff who spent months listening to me talk about a book on contracts. If that was not enough, he also proofread the manuscript multiple times, allowed me to take over his home office and has been my project manager throughout this process and in life. Finally, I dedicate this book to Asher and Parker, our greatest joys.

About the Author

Rachel Barnett is an experienced General Counsel who runs a legal department and is responsible for all aspects of the company's legal affairs. When Rachel first became in-house counsel, she was one of the youngest woman in a general counsel role of a publicly traded company. As General Counsel, Rachel manages a wide-range of legal matters for the company, including, among other things, corporate governance, employment, intellectual property, corporate transactions, securities compliance and general litigation. She has responsibility for reviewing, drafting and negotiating the legal terms of a broad range of commercial contracts. She also develops internal processes and provides training sessions to paper transactions from beginning to end. Rachel was recently elected to be a member of the board of directors.

Prior to going in-house, Rachel was an attorney in the Litigation department at Skadden, Arps, Slate, Meagher and Flom, LLP, where she specialized in representing corporations and their officers and directors in a variety of litigation matters, including merger and acquisition litigation, shareholder derivative lawsuits and securities fraud class actions at both the trial court and appellate levels.

In 2016, Rachel began co-teaching a course entitled "Exploring the Role of the General Counsel" at Columbia Law School along with the General Counsel of LVMH Moët Hennessy Louis Vuitton Inc. The course teaches students how to combine practical business sense with legal knowledge to achieve commercial objectives. The course is designed specifically to expose law students to real-world experience. Rachel sees this class as an opportunity to teach students about the inner workings of Corporate America through the eyes of in-house counsel.

Rachel earned her juris doctor degree from Columbia Law School and a Bachelor of Science degree from Cornell University. Rachel clerked for the Honorable Vice Chancellor Stephen P. Lamb of the Delaware Court of Chancery.

Table of Contents

A Short & Happy Guide to Business Contracts

CHAPTER 1

Introduction: Business Contracts Made Easy

The business team wants to enter into a commercial arrangement with another party, now what?

The knee-jerk reaction is to respond with "let's call the lawyer." Often times people think legal words are a foreign language that should be left solely to lawyers. You know, the ones who spent three years at law school and learned how to write legalese. When asked to review legal terms in a contract—let's admit it, most people tune out.

Perhaps there is a sense that non-lawyers are afraid to make a mistake. Without a lawyer's stamp of approval, they could accidentally sign away rights or expose the business to unknown risks and liabilities. It's this fear that makes many people lose sight of the simple fact that contracts are, and have always been, in their basic format simply words on paper. Let me say this another way: If you can read, there is no reason why you cannot understand a business contract. The words, which may seem foreign at first, can be learned by anyone who is willing to acquire a new skill.

1

Think of it this way: A commercial contract simply memorializes a business agreement between two parties and uses some fancy legal language to do so. If well written, the agreement will be straightforward, comprehensive and easily understood by non-lawyers and lawyers alike. Indeed, the underlying premise of preparing a contractual agreement is to draft a document that is, above all else, CLEAR. Arguably the single most important principle for contract drafting is for the contract to be clear enough so the average person would understand the terms of the deal. In a sense, parties would be better served if contracts were written using ordinary words in a form easy to understand.

Having said that, in reality, contracts nonetheless continue to include certain clauses that read like complicated jargon. This is probably because these clauses were drafted by artful lawyers centuries ago and remain in contracts to this day. Back in time, a lawyer wrote down convoluted language, which was then passed on to other lawyers, and, generations later, somehow made its way into every agreement. We are now left with clauses in contracts that are often misunderstood (even, while we hate to acknowledge it, by lawyers who continue to write them down). Why we cannot just use plain, ordinary words, or at least shorter sentences, would not be asking much.

More times than not, parties settle on contract terms that are ambiguous, leaving them exposed to potential conflicts down the road. In some cases, ambiguity in contracts is a result of inattentive drafting and both sides not paying enough attention to details. Stated bluntly, sometimes people are lazy. Other times, parties may have time constraints and want to close the deal so they overlook ambiguous language. "Let's move on!" Still further, parties can decide to strategically leave a particular provision unclear. For example, if a party knows the other side will likely not agree to its position if they drill down on the details, the party may tactically remain silent, leave the clause ambiguous and attempt to preserve an argument for down the road. Regardless of the reasons behind why contracts are not always drafted with the utmost of clarity, it's important to understand that uncertainty leads a party to risk and exposure. Unfortunately, expensive litigation can follow as a result.

The goal of this book is to provide you with a practical understanding of the critical components of a typical business contract. This book will teach you to be a better and clearer contract drafter, avoid common mistakes, and protect yourself or your company should a relationship sour or not live up to your initial expectations. Once you learn these archaic clauses and understand the reasoning behind them, you can apply your knowledge to a variety of business situations and perhaps avoid unexpected surprises later on. You will have a fuller appreciation of the deals you execute and be empowered to make contract negotiations work for you, not against you. This will, without a doubt, make life easier.

This book will help you understand the main clauses repeatedly found in business contracts. It would be impossible for me to explain every iteration of contract language you may come across in the business world. I will leave that for artificial intelligence one day. However, this book will provide helpful and useful insights regarding the most common terms in a typical business contract that are used on an everyday basis.

What most fail to realize is that a large number of business contracts contain routine legal clauses. There is no real secret sauce to general business contracts since, for the most part, they contain the same types of clauses. Yes, the cat is now officially out of the bag. Once you read about these common clauses, you will notice them applied in virtually every different industry, whether you are a small-business owner or work for a Fortune 500 company.

This book, importantly, focuses on combining legal topics with commercial sense and business realities. The following pages explain when you should push for certain terms and when you may be better off compromising. They will also inform you about contract language that can be tricky, and warn you when you should tread cautiously when agreeing to certain terms. This book is meant to be a practical guide with standard principles and a simplified framework to assist you with any type of business arrangement.

This book will make the contracting process easier for you. Instead of tuning out when you see legal language, this book will hopefully make you appreciate what you are agreeing to and remind you why you should care. Learning about customary terms found in business contracts will limit lawyer time, save on resources, and avoid unnecessary delays so you can move forward with your business and achieve your commercial objectives. Keep in mind, you can only protect yourself and your company once you know what you are signing.

The Point:

- Many business contracts contain the same types of clauses. You can become knowledgeable about these common clauses to help streamline the contract process and understand what is fair and reasonable.

- Once you grasp the primary clauses in business contracts, you will know what you are actually agreeing to with your counterparty and become a smarter negotiator.

- Learning about the key terms in a business contract will help you manage exposure to risk and be more efficient in negotiating contract terms, thereby saving time and legal costs.

CHAPTER 2

Top Terms in a Business Contract

Term and Termination Clauses

One of the most basic elements of a business contract is its term. A "term" clause in a business contract sets forth the duration of the parties' relationship. It states when the contract commences and how long the contract will remain in force—the beginning and the end. It's really that simple. The term will either (i) expire when time runs out; (ii) automatically renew; or (iii) be cut short by a party exercising a termination clause (as discussed in the following section).

A term provision typically looks like this:

This Agreement will begin on the date set forth above (the "Effective Date"), and will continue in full force and effect for one (1) year, unless terminated earlier by either Party in accordance with this Agreement.

Instead of specifying a particular commencement date, a contract can also be drafted to provide that the term begins on the date the contract is signed by the last party. Whatever the

7

"term" of the contract may be, you will want to understand how long you are bound with the counterparty in a legal contract and feel comfortable that the term suits your business needs. If you do not want to be bound by a legal agreement for a long term, then simply negotiate a shorter period.

However, if the counterparty insists on a long-term contract, there is another way you can protect yourself. As discussed in more detail in the termination section, you can push for a termination clause "for convenience" so you can get out of the contract for any reason (or no reason) prior to the term expiring. That way, you can agree to a longer commitment, perhaps even secure a good price for a while, but still have an exit strategy should you want a way out.

Beware of Automatic Renewals

When reviewing a term provision, watch out for extra language that provides the term will automatically renew. Put it this way, if you see the word "renew" in your agreement, you will want to understand this renewal obligation. This is especially true if the contract automatically renews and provides limited means for you to terminate the business arrangement (like those magazine subscriptions that pile up in your house that you forgot to cancel).

Here is the type of language that gets included in a template agreement, a favorite of companies that want to lock you in for many terms:

> *At the end of the Term, this Agreement will automatically renew for consecutive renewal terms of twelve (12) months, unless the consumer provides the merchant written notice not less than sixty (60) days prior to the end of the then current term.*

Stated simply, this clause means that you may be stuck paying for another twelve months of service if you do not cancel in time. More often than not, parties do not cancel their contracts before they auto renew. You probably have already experienced the frustration of agreeing to an auto renewal clause when you forgot to cancel your online subscriptions and have been stuck paying for services you no longer use.

Let's see how this plays out in the real world. After you sign the contract, you likely file it away and don't think about it for a while. You may remember that you signed on for a year service and have in the back of your mind to re-evaluate when nearing the end of the relationship. For example, let's say, to make it easy, you sign up for a new cable TV service on January 1st for a one-year term. Around December, as the year is coming to a close, you decide to switch TV service providers. If you send a notice to the cable TV provider that you are moving on, you will likely get a notice back stating otherwise. You will then be surprised to learn that you had to cancel at least 60 days prior to the term ending to avoid automatic renewal. The counterparty points out that you should have sent notice by November 1st and, thus, the contract has renewed for another year. You are left with your cable TV provider for another one-year term or have to negotiate your way out. In either case, you will be paying for this mistake. Stinks doesn't it?

The reality is that you don't tend to put a calendar entry for every contract you enter into to remind you to cancel the agreement before a certain date. If you do, then kudos for being so organized. However, for the rest of us, we are not even thinking about the term of a contract 60 days before the agreement expires. We may be focusing on other things, not whether there is a mechanism in place to stop automatic renewals.

So what do you do when you spot an automatic renewal clause? You can cross it out with a polite "no thank you" and "let's revisit our business partnership and mutually decide whether to continue the relationship after the term." Perhaps, like most of us, you are not interested in jumping through hoops to leave the business relationship. Alternatively, you can craft a renewal clause to require written consent before triggering a renewal of the agreement. In addition, you can ask to have the choice to decide (which in the legal world we say "in your sole discretion") whether to renew the term for additional periods. That way, you don't *have* to renew, but are provided an option to renew. If these options are rejected, at a minimum, you can demand that the other party provides you written notice prior to automatic renewal. In other words, ask for a reminder so you can cancel before the renewal date.

Ultimately, unless you benefit from being bound in a continuous business relationship, push for optionality to get out when the term expires. No need to stress about whether you have a calendar entry reminding you to send notice to stop an auto-renewal provision. In short, look out for the auto-renewals and avoid paying for a service you no longer need simply because you unintentionally missed the arbitrary deadline to cancel.

The Point:

- Watch out for automatic renewal clauses that can make it difficult to cancel a business relationship. These clauses can be hidden in language addressing the term of an agreement.

- If there is no clause in the contract permitting the agreement to be terminated for any reason whatsoever (known as a termination for convenience clause addressed below), be careful about agreeing to a rigid automatic renewal clause, as you can get stuck for another full term with no easy way out.

The Basics of a Termination Clause

An essential and very important provision in virtually all business contracts is the termination clause. Pay close attention to this clause. Basically, the termination clause sets forth how and under what circumstances a party can exit the agreement should it decide that the business relationship is not working. A termination clause provides a "way out."

It may seem odd to think about how to exit a business relationship when you are just commencing discussions with a party to work towards partnership. However, if you are contracting for the purpose of receiving a product or service, keep in mind that your business strategy may change over time and you may no longer want or need the service or product purchased. Moreover, a relationship may not always go according to plan. A problem could arise and the business might seek to exit the relationship quickly to avoid further liabilities and unexpected costs.

For a buyer of a product or service—Think of it this way: You don't want to be explaining to your boss why the company is still paying for a product or service that the company does not find satisfactory or that is not working to your initial expectations. If you can get out of the contract quickly and without much hassle, you can likely limit potential problems and avoid unnecessary losses.

For a seller of a product or service—Think of it this way: On the flip side, what if you are the company providing the product or service to a third party? You may have a different view and want to lock in the other party for a certain period of time, making it more difficult to terminate the relationship. It is possible that your company will be expending upfront resources, such as building technology solutions or purchasing components to assemble, as part of the partnership. You also want to get paid . . . for as long as possible. In effect, sellers often want predictability on collecting revenue.

As a seller, you don't want to be explaining to your boss why the company expended a substantial amount of resources toward a partnership, which was subsequently cancelled by the other party on short notice. Or, you don't want to deal with the other party shopping your price around and unexpectedly cancelling the contract should they find a better price elsewhere. If you are investing time (including legal time) and money (including legal costs) in a partnership, understand the termination clause and how easy the other party can exit the relationship.

To make it simple, there are basically two ways a contract can be terminated: (1) for convenience and (2) for cause.

Termination for Convenience

A termination for convenience clause essentially allows a party to exit the contract for any reason or no reason at all. The party seeking to terminate the agreement does not have to prove a failure or breach by the other party; but rather, it only has to notify the other party within the time frame stated in the provision. In other words, when the convenience clause is invoked, there is no need to argue over cause and responsibility, making it much easier to exit the relationship. Think of it as essentially negotiating an escape route. This is what a typical termination for convenience clause looks like:

> *This Agreement may be terminated by either Party at any time without cause, for any reason or for no reason, upon providing thirty days (30 days) prior written notice to the other Party.*

By having this clause in an agreement, it allows either party to terminate easily the agreement by providing a 30-day advance written notice to the other party. In general, the amount of notice provided to the other party before termination, in this case 30 days, can vary depending on the parties' relative circumstances.

Practically speaking, when you are negotiating time for providing prior notice, consider how long it will take to transition away from the partnership. If you are a seller of services, a longer notice provision provides more months of pay before the agreement is over. A buyer, on the other hand, is often left paying for the services during the notice period, even after it has let the other party know of its intention to exit the relationship.

Additionally, you will want to consider how terminating the relationship will unfold in practice. It can be undesirable, and, quite frankly awkward, to have several months left working together under the contract after providing notice of termination. Moreover, make sure to think about whether you will need cooperation from the counterparty to help transition to an alternative provider. If so, you will want to provide sufficient time to switch providers, and perhaps include language outlining the transition process. Also, make sure to be pleasant to the other side when issuing a termination letter, particularly if you are hoping for a smooth transition process and want to preserve your business reputation.

A termination for convenience provision is perhaps one of the most impactful provisions in a business contract. It essentially allows a party to seamlessly exit the business relationship without placing blame on the other party. If you do not negotiate a termination for convenience clause, you may have no easy way out of the business relationship. Instead, you can be left with a termination clause that has strict requirements, which can be hard to satisfy, in order to exit the contractual relationship. Without such a clause, the contract could require you to prove the opposing party materially breached the agreement in order to terminate the relationship. Put simply, you can be stuck. Thus, if there is a chance things will not work out, or you want to keep options open, you should consider protecting the business by negotiating a termination for convenience clause so you can exit the contract without conflict or blame.

On the other hand, if you are the one selling products or services, you may want to lock in the counterparty. You are probably inclined to not agree to a termination for convenience provision to ensure you have guaranteed revenue unless something goes wrong. It may be your intention to make it difficult for the other party to have a way out, especially if your business spent time and incurred expenses to partner with the counterparty. With that said, you may be willing to offer the other party a better price if it agrees to limit its termination rights. Thus, if you want to lock the other party into the business arrangement, you may reject a termination for convenience clause, offer a discount for a fixed term, or insist on a longer notice period to make it more difficult to withdraw from the relationship on short notice.

The Point:

- Whether you want the ability to exit the agreement or prefer locking your counterparty in to a certain period of time, carefully read the termination provision to confirm the language matches your preference.

- If you would like the ability to exit the relationship for any reason whatsoever, or no reason at all, negotiate a termination "for convenience" clause.

- Practically speaking, a termination for convenience clause makes a break-up of a business arrangement simpler and can be a saving grace should the business find out that the product or service does not meet expectations.

Termination for Cause

Nearly all commercial contracts allow a party to terminate the agreement if the other party fails to deliver what was promised and does not fix the situation within a certain period of time. Should a party mess up and not resolve the issue, it makes sense for the other party to terminate the business relationship. This concept is set forth in what is known as a "termination for cause" provision. Unlike a termination for convenience clause (which allows a party to exit the relationship for any reason or no reason at all), a termination for cause provision sets out specific circumstances upon which a party can terminate the contract, sometimes immediately.

Generally speaking, a buyer of products or services is better off with *both* a termination for convenience clause that allows the buyer to terminate for any reason after the notice period, as well as a termination for cause provision that prescribes a limited set of causes that could trigger a more immediate termination right. As mentioned above, a seller of products or services, conversely, wants to get paid longer and often times has more incentive to make it more difficult for the buyer to cancel the contract.

This is what a typical termination "for cause" clause looks like:

This Agreement may be terminated by either Party immediately upon notice to the other Party if the other Party: (a) materially breaches any of its obligations under this Agreement, which breach is not remedied within thirty (30) days following written notice to the breaching Party; (b) has a receiver or similar party appointed for its property, becomes insolvent, acknowledges its insolvency in any manner, ceases to do business, makes an assignment for the benefit of its creditors, or files a petition in bankruptcy; or (c) engages in any unlawful business practice related to that Party's performance under this Agreement.

Let's break it down. This provision essentially means that a party cannot exit the business relationship unless one of the following three things occurs. First, a party "materially" breaches the agreement and then, after proper notice, fails to cure the breach within 30 days. This is probably one of the most typical phrases in a termination for cause provision. But what does it really mean to "materially" breach a contract? At the outset, a party has to figure out what constitutes a "material" breach—which can often be murky and not straightforward.

A "material breach" essentially means that a party fails to perform under the contract, resulting in the other party not receiving the substantial benefit of the bargain. This is not a minor non-performance; it is a royal mess up that goes to the heart of the contract. Claiming a material breach can be a high threshold, and if uncertain, the right to terminate will be questioned. For example, defaulting on payments or stopping services altogether could be considered a "material" breach. But you would be surprised by how many in-between and unexpected problems occur that might leave you scratching your head. Indeed, if the other party offers to fix the problem, it will be even harder to claim the contract was "materially" breached and truly broken.

Put simply, it can, at times, be difficult to decipher whether what your counterparty failed to do is truly "material" to the agreement between the parties, thereby allowing you to invoke the termination for cause provision. To avoid this confusion, some parties insert language defining what exactly would constitute a material breach. Any attempt to avoid ambiguity by clarifying what is considered a "material" breach will provide more ease in understanding your rights to terminate for cause.

However, once you have figured out the "material" part, now you need to actually notify the counterparty of the breach and remind the counterparty that it has 30 days to remedy the matter. While this may sound simple, in practice, it can be frustrating. If your counterparty actually materially breaches an agreement, you may want the ability to exit the agreement right away. But, the termination for cause provision provides that the aggrieved party must give the defaulting party the opportunity to remedy its breach before proceeding to terminate. Thus, you have to provide written notice, wait and see if the other party can fix (or, in legal terms, we call it "cure") the matter, and, only after it fails to cure following 30 days, will you have cause to terminate the agreement. Ugh. When that happens, you will probably wish you had negotiated a termination for convenience clause to exit the contract without hassle.

The second part of the termination for cause provision typically involves language around a party becoming insolvent or heading towards bankruptcy. This is designed for the practical reason of allowing one party to cancel the contract when the counterparty appears to be on the verge of a major failure. For example, the counterparty is heading towards bankruptcy or insolvency whereby the party cannot pay its bills any longer. Most people want the option to terminate an agreement and not continue doing business with a counterparty that is about to go under.

Finally, the third part of the termination for cause provision provides a quick exit from the contract if the counterparty is engaging in illegal or unlawful actions. You do not want to be intertwined in a business relationship if the counterparty is acting unlawfully. For this reason, parties commonly include such termination language to allow them to get out immediately should this occur.

While you may come across a variety of other termination for cause particulars, the three addressed above are most commonly found in commercial contracts. This is for good reason. Situations where a party materially breaches the agreement, is heading for bankruptcy, or engages in unlawful misconduct are likely so serious that there is no question as to why the other party would want to terminate the legal relationship and end it fast.

The Point:

- It can be difficult to exit a business contract when you only have a provision that allows you to terminate for cause.

- This means you actually have to find cause, oftentimes even provide 30 days' notice and allow the counterparty to cure the problem, before you can exit the business relationship.

- If you are reviewing an agreement and are limited to a termination for cause only, you could be stuck in the business relationship for the entire term of the agreement or face a dispute over the presence of cause. To avoid such a situation, consider negotiating both termination for cause and termination for convenience clauses.

Keep an Eye Out for a Termination Penalty

When you are reading a termination provision, look out for language that requires you to continue to pay for services past the termination date or penalizes early termination of an agreement. Ideally, if you are purchasing a product or service, you probably desire to pay only for what is actually consumed until the date of termination. If you are paying on a monthly or yearly basis, you may want to consider adding language similar to the following:

Upon termination, Party will pay a pro-rated amount of the fee until the date of termination.

The foregoing language will save you from paying extra, such as for an entire month, if you ended the contract in the beginning of the month. Moreover, if you set up payment terms so that you pay in advance, be specific that you will receive a refund of the pro-rated amount upon termination. When this is not made clear, you can be left paying for services or products that you are no longer using. Without explicit language promising a refund, you risk not getting your money back.

Sometimes, you may come across language that essentially requires you to pay a monetary penalty if you exercise your right to terminate the agreement early. For example, you may come across a provision such as the following:

If the services are terminated by the other Party prior to completing the term applicable thereto, then fifty-percent (50%) of the unpaid balance remaining under this Agreement with respect to the applicable term becomes due and payable in a lump sum.

Generally speaking, be wary about these types of penalty provisions, as they can effectively undercut and even prevent you from exercising your right to terminate the contract. You may have worked hard to negotiate a fair exit clause, but now this harsh penalty clause changes the equation on whether you decide to terminate. In the above clause, you would be on the hook to pay half of the unpaid remaining balance upon termination. But, what if you want to terminate in the first month because the services were not what you initially expected? Practically speaking, the chance of exercising your termination right early on is unlikely, given that you will not want to dole out 50% of the remaining balance. Footing such a bill upfront is expensive and can be an unpleasant outcome.

The point is that having a termination fee, especially one that feels like a punishment, can undermine your right to terminate in the first place. On the other hand, this should not come as a surprise since the purpose of the termination fee is to encourage a party to honor the contract for its full duration. If a deal is a deal, then you may be thinking, why should a party be able to cancel early without paying a price? Including a termination fee may not be so bad.

For example, you may want a clean break if things do not work out. It could be beneficial to negotiate a flat cancellation fee that makes sense economically should parties decide to go their separate ways. One party may have upfront costs and resources they are investing to provide services and seek a termination fee to cover those costs should the contract end early. The other party may agree to a termination fee in exchange for the ability to easily exit the agreement prematurely.

Regardless of whether you think termination fee provisions are good or bad, it is important that you spot them in the agreement and make the decision for yourself—rather than be blindsided later on when you attempt to cancel the agreement while the other side is seeking a pay day.

The Point:

- Think hard before agreeing to a termination penalty. The payment amount can be expensive and undermine your ability to terminate the contract.

Survival Clause

What happens after termination or expiration of an agreement? Generally speaking, a party's rights only last for the length of the contract period. Upon termination, all rights and obligations of the parties can be extinguished unless stated otherwise. A well-written business contract, however, will plan ahead and set forth the clauses that logically should survive after termination. Responsibilities and obligations should not always stop upon contract termination, since events can transpire after the contract ends. In what is known as a "survival clause," parties typically specify which contractual clauses will remain in effect after the termination or expiration of the agreement.

If you forget to include a survival clause, you will be left in a frustrating situation should a problem arise after the contract expires or terminates. For example, without a survival clause, it could be unclear whether the predetermined dispute resolution clause detailing how disputes will be handled still applies. A party could go against the agreed upon location (or venue) for disputes and commence litigation elsewhere. Moreover, consider whether any payments could possibly be owed after termination. You do not want to lose out on any unpaid payment obligations that become due after termination. Also, what if a third-party lawsuit arises after the agreement terminates? The party facing the lawsuit may no longer be indemnified for third-party claims. A party may seek to avoid an indemnity obligation if the contract fails to note that such provision survives termination of the agreement. The party seeking indemnification can be left exposed.

There are a number of provisions a party may want to continue after termination, such as: indemnification (protect yourself if a claim surfaces later); confidentiality (maintain your secrets even after the contract ends); limitation of liability (exposure limitations continuing after contract terminates); data security (keeping data safe after the relationship is over); payment (to the extent payment is due after contract ends); dispute resolution (handling disputes arising later); and miscellaneous (boilerplate language still governs the relationship after termination). It is also standard for certain representations and warranties to continue after termination.

A typical survival clause will look like the following:

The provisions covering Payment (Section 2), Indemnification (Section 5), Confidentiality (Section 6), Termination (Section 9), Limitation of Liability (Section 10); Dispute Resolution (Section 12), Governing Law and Venue (Section 14), and Miscellaneous (Section 16) shall survive termination or expiration of this Agreement.

In practice, some practitioners may just list the section numbers, without the title names, which survive past termination. This can lead to mistakes as section numbers can change in negotiations when parties mark up agreements. You certainly do not want to be left exposed without indemnification surviving termination because you carelessly included the wrong section number. Thus, it is best practice to both reconfirm that the survivorship clause is accurate after the terms are finalized and to include the name of the headings to avoid any misunderstandings.

Additionally, if you want to protect yourself from forgetting a provision that you would like to continue after termination, you can add the following language:

Rights and obligations under this Agreement which by their nature should survive will remain in effect after termination or expiration of this Agreement.

This language provides extra added protection to demonstrate that the parties intended those provisions that logically should continue to survive termination. Although, how a court ultimately interprets that language and decides on which provisions survive may be murky.

Lastly, while it is not as common in business contracts, parties can set forth a particular time period for survival, instead of leaving it indefinite. For example, a party may include language that:

This Section (Confidentiality) shall survive for three (3) years following the expiration or early termination of the Agreement.

If parties can agree on a time frame, this can result in greater clarity and certainty for the survival of the parties' rights.

The Point:

- Do not forget to include a survival clause in a business contract, otherwise your rights will be extinguished at the termination or expiration of the agreement.

- Double check prior to executing the document that the survival clause accurately states which sections will survive termination, as section numbers can get rearranged during negotiations.

Recitals

Parties commonly include preliminary paragraphs to a contract with fancy legal language as if they are setting the scene and putting forth some sort of formal introduction. These paragraphs, which begin with "WHEREAS" clauses, typically precede the main legal provisions in the agreement. It is easy to locate this language, often referred to as "recitals," since the format is almost always the same. Essentially, the paragraphs look like this:

WHEREAS, Party A is engaged in the business of [insert description of business]; and

WHEREAS, Party B desires to obtain Party A's services for the [insert commercial purpose] to be undertaken in accordance with the terms of this Agreement.

NOW, THEREFORE, in consideration of the mutual promises contained herein and for good and valuable consideration, the receipt and sufficiency of which are hereby acknowledged, the Parties agree as follows:

Do You Really Need Recitals?

Recitals can provide context for why parties are entering into a business relationship. They are intended to be, and are often viewed as, providing background information. Recitals can lay out the purpose and intent for entering into the agreement and set forth any prior history between parties.

The problem with these preamble clauses is that, for the most part, they do not create legally binding obligations on a party. In fact, recitals are often not considered part of the contract unless expressly incorporated therein. Thus, a party wants to be careful that it is not mistakenly relying on language in recitals, which may have no legal effect. In other words, don't depend on any representations or promises set forth in a recital alone. The general rule is that a party should ensure all legal rights and obligations are set forth in the main body of the contract. Alternatively, should recitals include important information, parties should expressly incorporate the recitals by reference in the main text of the agreement.

Recitals are not supposed to create legally binding rights (unless the contract expressly says so); however, they can be used by courts to provide context around the business relationship.

Recitals may assist a decision maker in deciphering the intention of the parties should the main contract language be unclear and ambiguous.

In practice, should a dispute arise, a party may latch on to language in a WHEREAS clause to argue it supports that party's interpretation of a term in the contract. For example, a party could claim "Your Honor, my position holds more water, the parties intended for X, and this was confirmed in the WHEREAS clauses. Therefore, I should win this dispute." Given this, recitals are not totally meaningless and should be reviewed and checked for accuracy. With that said, how much weight a court will ultimately give to a WHEREAS clause is hard to know. The main body of the contract will likely take precedence over any background recital clause.

As a further matter, in reality, neither party nor its attorneys pay close attention to these introductory paragraphs in the first place. We typically skim the "WHEREAS" clauses and move on to the heart of the agreement, which is what really matters. Some might argue that it's time to retire recitals.

The Point:

- Recitals are not the place to put legal rights or obligations, rather all key terms should be inserted in the body of the contract, or, if necessary, recitals should be expressly incorporated into the operative provisions.

- Avoid relying on language that is inserted in a recital alone, as it may not be binding and may have no legal effect.

- Nonetheless, keep in mind that a party may point to recitals should a dispute arise to demonstrate the intention of the parties—so pay attention, check for accuracy, and don't ignore them.

Payment Terms

The payment terms in an agreement address the parties' negotiation of how and when a party will pay the other for the purchase of goods or services. The payment clause specifies the amount, or a formula for calculating the amount, of payments or fees owed under the agreement.

There are a variety of different payment terms parties can discuss. A typical payment provision will address what type of payments were negotiated. This may include an hourly, monthly or yearly fee, lump sum payment, revenue share or other alternative payment structure. The payment provision will also cover when payment is due to the other party, which could provide that it is due upon signing of the agreement, or within 30 days following the receipt of a product or service. It could potentially include a subscription payment due on certain monthly or annual dates.

A payment clause may also address the payment method chosen between parties, such as whether payment will be made by direct deposit, check, wire transfer, or other method. A payment provision can specify which currency applies, such as all prices are in U.S. dollars and payments shall be in U.S. currency.

A standard payment provision is straightforward and looks like this:

Party A shall pay Party B a monthly fee of five-thousand dollars ($5,000). Unless otherwise indicated, all payments shall be due within thirty (30) days of the date of the invoice. Party A shall pay all amounts due under this Agreement at the address set forth in Section X of this Agreement or such other location as Party B *designates in writing. All monetary amounts shall be paid in the currency of United States dollars.*

Not all payment provisions have simplistic terms; payment provisions are often more detailed. Parties can agree on complex formulas, which can be premised on fluctuating prices, quantity amounts and other factors, depending on the business arrangement. For example, parties may agree on a sliding scale whereby the buyer receives a discounted price based on the volume of goods purchased from the seller. Another example is a take-or-pay contract, often found in energy supply contracts, where a buyer can either take specified quantities of a product from the supplier at the contract price or pay the supplier a fee. Parties could also seek to lock in the price with a fixed payment schedule. Moreover, if a party is contracting for services, it may structure payment terms based on specific milestones that must be achieved before payment is due.

Regardless of what form a payment clause provides, you will want to confirm it is clear and sets forth the parties' agreement on price and how money will be transferred. Make sure the payment clause details exactly how much is to be paid, when the payment is to be made and the method for making payment. Moreover, it is best practice to write out in plain English the amount agreed upon, as set out above, stating "five-thousand dollars ($5,000)". And, of course, don't forget to double check that the words coincide with the numerical amount, and that the payment amount matches the parties' negotiated and agreed upon price.

The Point:

- A payment clause should be simple and straightforward. It plainly sets forth how one party will pay the other for goods or services purchased.

- A payment clause should be customized to include the type of payment arrangement, the mechanics of how payments will be made and the timing for when payments are due.

What to Watch Out for in a Payment Clause

While payment terms themselves are often straightforward, added language can lead to problems. The below sets forth gotcha language for unsuspecting parties.

Modifying Prices. You want to be careful not to agree to any payment clause that allows the seller to change the agreed-upon price without your permission. If you are a buyer of a product or service, watch out for language that allows the seller to *"review and modify the fees at its discretion."* Any language that allows a party to modify prices without first obtaining the other party's written consent should be scrutinized and treated with caution.

Practically speaking, what is the point of agreeing to a price if the seller inserts language stating it can revise the price later on? You might as well hand over a blank check. It is highly unlikely the price is going down. Unless you are fine with the seller increasing prices during the term, consider crossing out any language that allows a seller to modify, revise or amend the pricing schedule without your written consent. Generally speaking, when parties negotiate prices in a business contract, such prices should not be modified unless through a formal amendment process (as discussed later on), requiring agreement from both sides.

With that said, there may be certain exceptions where permitting a party to modify prices makes business sense. Sometimes a contract will provide that a party can amend prices with 30 days prior notice, and, if the other party does not like the payment increase, it can promptly terminate the agreement. Such language can seem unreasonable at first glance. But, this type of language may be appropriate if it relates to a renewal term. In other words, a seller may explain: "We are committed to the fees for the duration of the initial term, and it is only after this time period that we need to reserve the right to revise prices, including if our costs go up unexpectedly." In other words, for longer-term contracts, a party may desire the flexibility after the initial term to charge current rates.

On the other hand, if you are a buyer and expect to maintain the business relationship for a while, you may consider negotiating for yourself an option to renew with no price increase or a minimal price increase. Trust me, you can be better off negotiating the price ahead of time for a renewal term than waiting until your counterparty raises prices after you are enjoying its services. Depending on the industry, you may be able to negotiate pre-determined prices with (i) a zero percent increase or (ii) the lesser of 2% or the rate of inflation for a second or third term. This will protect you from having to renegotiate prices later on or confronting a price hike after you become dependent on a particular supplier.

If you negotiated a flexible renewal provision, you may be able to choose not to renew, terminate the agreement and request a lower price in the rare event that a seller's prices go down. Thus, you have much to gain and not much to lose if you can negotiate the option to renew at the same or similar price.

Unreasonable Expenses. In addition to payments owed, certain service providers will want to be reimbursed for expenses incurred while working for a client. These expenses can relate to travel and transportation, such as hotels, airfare, car rental, meals, etc. If you fail to set boundaries on how expenses can be charged, the bill can add up quickly.

One way to protect yourself against sticker shock from an invoice of incurred expenses is to require the other party to obtain consent before charging expenses. This type of language looks like this: *"All travel and other expenses incurred by Party A must be pre-approved in writing by Party B (email approval being acceptable) prior to being billed to Party B."* In practice, email notice should suffice, as it may be inefficient and unrealistic to require a more formal notice process for charging expenses. If, however, the circumstances are such that it is not practical to request consent before incurring expenses, try agreeing to a maximum amount that can be charged and requiring consent for any expenses incurred above that amount. You can also consider capping total expenses, stating that: *"in no event shall reimbursable expenses exceed fifteen thousand dollars ($15,000)."*

Furthermore, if you are concerned about the other party's careless spending behavior, you can add language requiring that all expenses must be *"authorized, ordinary and necessary out-of-pocket expenses reasonably incurred."* You can also require that all travel be booked through your company or in accordance with its travel and expense policy (which should then be attached to the agreement as an exhibit). Feel free to also throw in that you will only reimburse for coach airfare, and no expensive Bordeaux.

Upfront Billing. Every once in a while, you will come across an agreement that sets out upfront billing and provides a buyer will pay the seller upon execution of the agreement before receiving the products or services. This may make sense if the seller has upfront costs and requires payment at the time of signing to cover those costs. One thing to keep in mind is that if you pay a large sum upon signing of the agreement, it can be more difficult to terminate the agreement and get a refund should things not work out. If you are the buyer, practically speaking, it is not easy to claw back your money. Certain companies recognize this and will front load payments to reduce the leverage the other party has to withhold payments should there be a problem.

Speaking practically, it is much easier to dispute an invoice than to request a refund once you have paid. Thus, before agreeing to pay money upfront, you will want to be certain that the counterparty will deliver the goods or services as promised. If you ultimately decide to pay upfront, keep in mind that, in practice, it will be more difficult to recover money if the relationship sours.

Waiver of Payment Disputes. Payment clauses may include language that any dispute relating to payments must be raised within a certain period of time, otherwise it is waived or forfeited. In other words, a party is letting you know that you must raise any payment disputes by the stated deadline or you cannot seek recovery later on. Such language is not so common, and you should consider the consequences of agreeing to this restriction. This type of language can look like this:

Any dispute regarding payment from a Party hereunder must be submitted to the other Party in writing within thirty (30) days from the date of the relevant invoice or such dispute shall be deemed waived.

On one hand, one party may favor this language as it provides certainty that any dispute regarding payment will be raised within 30 days. This allows, for example, a party receiving payments to deny providing refunds after the deadline. It also forces the other party to raise any disputes promptly without delay. Moreover, companies may require certainty regarding payment collections for accounting reasons. The need for payment certainty may be tied to the company's revenue recognition.

On the other hand, the other party can be disadvantaged by this language. Practically speaking, a party may not realize a payment mistake until after the 30-day deadline. Now that party is stuck eating the costs because of this arbitrary deadline. If you are the party with more to lose, you likely want to cross out this language and not waive any of your rights relating to payment disputes. In the alternative, you can consider extending the time to dispute an invoice from 30 days to 90 days or beyond. Sometimes a party may ask for a period as long as 13 months to allow the party to confirm payments after it completes its year-end accounting. Ultimately, if you cannot eliminate the language altogether, negotiate a time period that gives sufficient time to review the bill, discover any inaccuracy and notify the other side.

Interest Owed for Delayed Payment. Often found in payment provisions is language that late payments will be charged interest against the payments owed. A late payment fee is typical, as it provides incentives for a party to pay on time and not ignore invoices. Thus, it is not uncommon to see provisions for late fees and interest charges in contracts. A purchaser, however, will want to read carefully such language and confirm that (i) the interest rate is reasonable under the circumstances and (ii) late payments only apply to amounts not in dispute.

Commercial contracts commonly set forth around a 1% to 2% monthly interest rate for payments that are overdue by 30 days or more. Should a commercial contract set a monthly interest rate that is egregious, such as above 10%, it would likely be struck down under state laws. Certain states have statutes that prohibit unreasonable interest rate charges for money owed. For this reason, you may see language to protect against a late fee provision being voided under applicable law. For example, a contract may state:

Late payments will be subject to an interest charge of the lesser of one and one-half percent (1.5%) per month or the highest rate permitted by applicable law.

When you glance over this provision, make sure to check that it has the word "lesser" and not "greater", or you may be on the hook for the maximum interest rate allowed under applicable state law. Yikes!

Moreover, interest charges on late payments should not apply if the amount claimed due is in dispute. You certainly do not want a seller to be charging you interest when you disagree with the invoiced amount. To avoid this, it is typical to include that interest would only be due on "undisputed" amounts following a default payment. Parties may go further specifying that:

This provision on charging interest on late payments shall not apply if the buyer has disputed an invoice in good faith.

Finally, often times in practice, a party will not enforce a late fee payment provision. If a party is a few weeks late, it is unlikely that the seller will threaten interest charges. Charging late fees can rub a business partner the wrong way. Moreover, since it is not always enforced, some parties can negotiate at the outset eliminating late payment interest charges altogether. If a purchaser has good credit and has conducted business with the seller before, it will have more bargaining leverage to argue against any interest charges for late payments. Practically speaking, whether a party charges a late payment fee is not typically a heavily negotiated term in a business contract.

Pay-for-Performance/Audit Rights. Depending on the business relationship, you may agree to a payment provision conditioned on the performance of a party. This can be in the form, for example, of a commission or a revenue-split. In particular, Internet companies often negotiate agreements based on performance metrics. It is common to execute agreements where you get paid for a party clicking on an advertisement, such as a cost-per-click ("CPC") arrangement, or when a consumer purchases a good or service online, a cost-per-acquisition ("CPA").

In circumstances where payment is based on the performance of a party, you will want to consider who is tracking the party's performance. You may decide to have an independent third party perform the tracking or you may trust the counterparty to keep its own tracking. If you go the latter route, you probably want to ask for audit rights. An audit provision provides a party the opportunity to review the books and records of the other party to confirm payments due are accurate.

A basic audit provision looks like the following:

Party A reserves the right to perform a limited and reasonable audit to verify payment amounts due hereunder and Party B agrees to cooperate with such audit and provide the requested documentation.

You may also find in an agreement an audit provision that is longer and more specific as to the process and procedures of the audit. The audit provision can set out how many times each year a party can request an audit and who has to perform the audit. For example, it could state that the party's representatives can conduct the audit or require an independent third party (such as an accounting firm) to conduct it. This type of provision can look like this:

Party B agrees that Party A and its authorized representatives or agents (collectively the "Auditing Party") reserves the right, at its own expense, to inspect, copy and audit any records of Party B directly relating to its payments made hereunder. Party B shall make all such facilities, records, personnel, books, accounts, data, reports, papers, and computer records available to the Auditing Party for the purpose of conducting such inspections and audits. Any such audit will be conducted at mutually agreed upon times, upon reasonable prior written notice (no less than ten (10) business days), and in a manner designed to minimize any disruption of Party B's normal business activities.

In addition, you may come across language in an audit provision that provides a party will pay for the audit if the auditing party discovers errors in the opposing party's payment calculation. Often times, a party will put a percentage on the error, like the opposing party will pay for the expenses of an audit if the party is 5% off in its payment calculation. Such language looks like this:

In the event the audit reveals an underpayment of five percent (5%) or more, Party B will pay the reasonable costs of the audit along with the amount of the underpayment.

Moreover, you could also find a penalty attached, on top of paying for the expense of the audit, should a party be caught making a mistake, or worse, cheating on the payment calculation. While these are common in audit provisions, a party that could be faced with an audit wants to make sure the percentage difference and any penalty charged are reasonable under the circumstances.

In practice, an audit provision is a useful tool, should a payment dispute arise. If you are trusting the other party to report its performance metrics, you are better off having audit rights as an option should you suspect payment inaccuracies. Another way to look at this is that, if you don't have audit rights, you can request the documentation and the other party can say "no thanks." Or, the party may cherry pick what documents it wants to share and you may not understand the full picture. When this happens, you are not in a great position. You will have to decide whether you want to do nothing, seek to terminate the agreement, or claim the other party is ripping you off and breaching the agreement. Starting down the path of claiming a breach of contract is not a pleasant experience.

In practice, it can be much easier to point to a pre-negotiated audit provision and request inspection of relevant documents. When you bring up the provision, you will be surprised to see, if your intuition was right, how quickly the billing dispute gets resolved. Without audit rights, you can be left with a steep hill to climb should a payment dispute arise.

Limitation of Liability

It is no secret to lawyers that a contract's limitation of liability clause needs to be taken seriously. In practice, if your counterparty breaches the contract, you will seek to get paid for any losses that you have incurred and will potentially continue to incur. You will ask yourself: "How can I recover my damages suffered after the counterparty failed to perform as promised?" The first thing you will want to review is the limitation of liability clause, which addresses what damages can be recouped.

As its name suggests, the clause provides a "limitation" on the amount and type of damages a party can recover from a breaching party. The purpose of a limitation of liability clause is to *limit* the damages owed to a party for losses suffered due to a breach of contract. In a limitation of liability clause, parties are setting the boundaries of what each can be liable for based on the business relationship. Parties are also limiting the scope of recoverable damages. If you fail to negotiate a fair and balanced limitation of liability clause, you will have to live with the ramifications should there be a dispute down the road.

A limitation of liability clause often contains two parts. The first part excludes entirely certain damages that can be recovered. The second part caps the amount of damages you could get paid from the breaching party. Pay close attention to a limitation of liability clause in any agreement you sign. It can substantially and single-handedly reduce a party's pay out when that party violates the agreement, leaving you exposed and incurring losses that are not recoverable.

Keep in mind, the party that insists on using its own contract template (typically the party supplying the products or services) often attempts to exclude as much liability as possible. This means that the party would rather not pay out, even for its own mistakes, presuming it can contract away its liability exposures.

To help you locate the limitation of liability clause, it is the clause that is almost always in ALL CAPS in an agreement. If you are asking why these provisions are in ALL CAPS, it is because the clause is important enough that courts and lawyers want the parties to actually read and pay attention to the language. They are purposefully making the clause conspicuous so that the non-breaching party cannot complain when it realizes, after the fact, it will not recoup all of its losses should a breach occur. It allows the breaching party to say, "How did you not notice that clause? It was in ALL CAPS!"

With that said, sometimes ALL CAPS language can have practically the opposite effect. People have become so accustomed to seeing this ALL CAPS paragraph that they now glaze over the language thinking it is a bunch of boilerplate legalese. But, before you ignore the ALL CAPS, let's better understand what this legal language means and the consequences for brushing it aside. This can be a BIG DEAL.

For starters, let's review the two parts of a limitation of liability clause:

Part I: You Cannot Recover from All Damages Suffered After a Breach

In the first part of a limitation of liability clause, a party is agreeing to limit its own recovery by waiving particular damages it could incur if the counterparty commits a breach. The party is saying: "I will not hold you accountable for certain losses that may occur because you failed to perform under the agreement." The counterparty naturally prefers this clause. Who wouldn't favor a clause that starts off with "you shall not be liable to the other party for [insert] damages", even when you were the one who made the mistake?

You may be thinking, why would anyone agree to limit their recovery when the other party failed to perform as promised? The honest truth is that a buyer may not realize the consequences of a limitation of liability clause or does not have bargaining leverage to shift more risk to the supplier. Having said that, the party who supplies a product or service does not want to be exposed to unlimited liability. A breach of contract can expose a party to various types of losses and the breaching party often is not willing to assume such risk. What's important to realize is that, in many situations, the value of the contract can be substantially lower than the liability exposures of a party.

Take, for example, a supplier who is selling a bag of screws for $9.99 to a manufacturer of paper products. The manufacturer uses the screws in one of its paper machines only to discover that a screw was defective and the machine breaks. The manufacturer is left incurring substantial losses, including $10,000 to replace the machine, thousands of dollars of lost profits with less paper products to sell and also, perhaps, reputational damages, as word gets out about the accident. You can bet the supplier of the $9.99 screws does not want to be responsible for all of these losses. If the supplier was a small business owner, this single defective screw could put the party out of business. Rather, the seller merely wants to provide a refund, replace the screw and nothing more. This is why the seller insisted on a limitation of liability clause that drastically limited the manufacturer's recovery for losses.

So, what exactly can the manufacturer recover from this failure? The answer depends on what the limitation of liability clause says. Generally speaking, if a party messes up and breaches the agreement, it is common for a breaching party to take responsibility for losses that would naturally occur as a direct result of the breach. These are called "direct" damages. They are essentially the ordinary and probable damages that a party will pay because they are reasonable and typical for the type of arrangement. For example, the manufacturer in the above example was directly damaged by the $9.99 that it spent on defective screws, and potentially purchasing new screws from another supplier. You want your money back.

A limitation of liability clause, however, can be designed to exclude everything else. Specifically, it is common to find in a limitation of liability clause language that the parties will not pay for any *other* types of damages that are not considered direct damages. These often include indirect damages, special damages, consequential damages, incidental damages and punitive damages (as described in the next section). Given that a party wants to avoid exposures to large liabilities, such as replacing a machine, lost profits, and reputational damages, a party can exclude these particular types of damages. This is known as a consequential damages disclaimer, which, if mutual, can look like this:

IN NO EVENT SHALL A PARTY BE LIABLE TO THE OTHER PARTY FOR ANY INDIRECT, SPECIAL, CONSEQUENTIAL, INCIDENTAL, OR PUNITIVE DAMAGES, RELATING TO ANY OBLIGATION UNDER THIS AGREEMENT, WHETHER OR NOT

INFORMED IN ADVANCE OF THE POSSIBILITY OF SUCH DAMAGES AND REGARDLESS OF THE FORM OF OR THEORY OF RELIEF OF ANY CLAIM OR ACTION.

What does this mean? In essence, parties are signalling to each other that they do not want to be responsible for indirect, special, consequential, incidental and punitive damages. These are types of damages beyond those considered "direct" damages. These types of damages are more removed, and may be considered one or two links down the chain. Let's take a closer look at these types of damages.

Indirect or Special or Consequential Damages. Often referred to together as "consequential damages", and used interchangeably in practice, these types of damages encompass liabilities that are more tangential. While they can be foreseeable, they may not be intended by the parties to be recoverable at the time the agreement was entered into. These "indirect, special or consequential damages" are considered one-step removed from ordinary direct damages. They may be damages suffered as a result of a breach because of the injured party's particular circumstances. They are often considered additional losses above and beyond the value of the bargained for goods or services. Such losses can include lost profits, loss of business opportunities, loss of goodwill, and reputational damages.

If this explanation still seems confusing, you are not alone. Truth be told, it can be difficult to differentiate between direct damages and these other types of damages.

For example, a party may have contracted to pay $500 to receive several gallons of paint. Relying on the paint to be delivered on time, the party executed a separate, non-cancellable agreement with a contractor to pay $1,000 a day for a team of painters to arrive on Wednesday. Should the paint be delayed until Friday, the paint company will claim that the $2,000 owed to the contractor for the two days without paint is considered consequential damages and cannot be recovered. In other words, the paint company will not take responsibility for how its breach (*i.e.*, delayed delivery) impacted others down the road.

In practice, it is often challenging to fully pin down what actually constitutes "consequential" damages, an often blurry concept. Unfortunately, it is one of those legal terms parties do not fully contemplate, yet commonly agree to blanket waivers of consequential damages. After a breach occurs, the non-breaching party is often surprised to learn that it cannot recover its full losses because it waived recoupment of consequential damages. Other times, parties disagree on what actually constitutes consequential damages that were waived by the parties. This leads to parties arguing in front of a judge, based on the particularized facts, what was meant by excluding "consequential" damages. But, even courts can differ on what is considered consequential damages and what is or is not recoverable under the contract. Sigh.

You can understand how confusion may arise based on another simple example: Let's say you purchase a photo from your counterparty for $50. Your plan is to use the photo in your new marketing platform that is set to be displayed in a few days. Indeed, you bought a $2,000 newspaper ad to display this beautiful picture and you were planning to reap thousands of dollars in profits from your advertisement. On the day your advertisement is set to run, you find out from your counterparty that there are problems with the photo. Your counterparty tells you that it does not have the rights to the photo. The party says it is truly sorry, but you cannot display the photo that you purchased in your upcoming advertisement.

Given this unfortunate situation, you go back and look at your agreement. It is probably obvious to you that you can get back your $50, as you were directly damaged by that amount. What may be less clear is whether you can seek the $2,000 newspaper advertisement fee, or the thousands of dollars in profits you lost by not displaying the advertisement. Those losses could be considered a consequence of the breach, and are in addition to the direct damage of $50.

Your recovery may not be entirely known. It is surely possible that a court may award you some of those damages. Don't you love when a lawyer tells you that it is difficult to draw clear lines and depends on the judge and the court? But, what is more likely to occur is that your counterparty will argue that it will take responsibility for paying you back for the photo and provide you a replacement photo. The other stuff is consequential damages, which the parties agreed could not be recovered.

The counterparty will say: "That is your particular problem, not mine. I am not paying your ad fee or lost profits." You may respond: "But I told you explicitly that I was relying on you for this photo to run my advertisement and this was important to my business." Your counterparty may not care. It can take the position that those losses were special to you and your individual circumstances and are not recoverable. The primary purpose of the contract was to supply a photo. The advertisement was tangential to that purpose. You are left frustrated by the course of events, and the mere $50 refund while you incur losses in the thousands.

In practice, however, the conversation may become more civil if the parties want to preserve the business relationship. The parties may not want to litigate in court or get lawyers involved. In reality, the first phone call to the lawyer could cost more than the potential cost to rectify the matter. The parties may choose to resolve the matter amicably by negotiating a compromised business resolution.

Incidental Damages. Incidental damages are commercially reasonable expenses incurred by one party as a result of the other party's breach of the contract. It refers to certain costs that a non-breaching buyer incurs if the goods are non-conforming. Alternatively, it can refer to costs that a non-breaching seller incurs if the goods are wrongfully rejected.

For example, consider a situation where a party ships a defective product in breach of the contract. As a result, the buyer ends up paying for storage fees while it waits for the other party to retrieve the defective product. These storage fees are considered incidental damages. On the flip side, incidental damages to an aggrieved seller include any expenses incurred in connection with the return of the goods, such as the cost of transporting them.

Practically speaking, it is common for incidental damages to be excluded from recovery in a limitation of liability clause. Indeed, incidental damages are almost always listed as an exclusion in a limitation of liability clause. With that said, parties should consider their particular situation and whether it makes sense to exclude or waive these types of damages. You will want to think carefully about whether incurring incidental damages under the circumstances is a possibility should a breach occur. If you desire to recover incidental damages, then cross it out of the damages waiver clause. Don't just glance over the blanket waiver and forfeit your rights unnecessarily.

Punitive Damages. These are damages that are awarded to punish the other party for acting in bad faith and breaching the agreement. It is common for a commercial arrangement to disallow the other party to seek punitive damages and there is good reason for this. Should you end up breaching an agreement, you may be comfortable paying out the direct damages you caused, but you certainly do not want to be punished.

What Else Are You Waiving in a Limitation of Liability Clause?

Sometimes you may come across additional, more specific, language eliminating recovery for certain losses. For example, a limitation of liability clause may explicitly state that the counterparty will not pay for "lost profits" or "loss of revenue" or be responsible for "loss of data" or "business interruption." Additionally, it may list other types of damages that could arise if the counterparty fails to perform its side of the deal. The reason for this is simple. The party is making known that it does not want to pay for these losses.

A party explicitly lists these types of losses because they may not be considered by a court as consequential damages that are waived under the limitation of liability clause. As discussed above, there can be a gray area of what is considered consequential damages and thereby not recoverable under a contract with a general consequential damages disclaimer. The line between direct damages that can be recouped and consequential damages that can be waived is often blurry and unpredictable. Therefore, the party is essentially saying: "I am not interested in a large dose of uncertainty and am explicitly telling you what I will not pay for should I fail to perform under the agreement." The party spells out the specific categories of damages that cannot be recovered by the other side—it does not want to leave it to a dispute or a courtroom fight later on.

Generally speaking, excluding these types of damages in a limitation of liability clause is commonly found in business contract templates, but it may not be appropriate for you based on your situation. Your counterparty typically does not want to be on the hook for such indirect damages for the simple reason that they can be very costly to pay out. Similarly, you may not want to be on the hook for these damages. They can be big-ticket items.

For example, if you disclose consumer sensitive data to a marketing agency and that agency is hacked because it does not have secure systems, you can expect the agency to attempt to disclaim liability. The marketing agency will likely maintain that the losses from the data breach, such as lost profits and reputational damages, are consequential damages and were expressly listed as not recoverable. You are left with escalating losses, no reimbursement for lost profits and reputational harm from the data breach. Perhaps even wishing you had read the limitation of liability clause more carefully. Had you spotted the risk ahead of time, you could have insisted on more coverage and not waived your right to recover certain damages. One option would have been to carve out confidentiality breaches entirely from the limitation of liability clause. Now it is too late.

Ultimately, a standard limitation of liability clause a party (especially a vendor) includes in its template barring recovery of certain types of losses can have real repercussions. Regardless of how your counterparty values the contract, you will want to allocate the risk exposure you believe is appropriate under your circumstances. Give thought to the potential harm presented by the product or service, and clarify which losses are recoverable under the agreement. Bargain hard for a more balanced and fair limitation of liability clause. If the counterparty will not initially budge on these terms, keep trying.

Are You Paying Close Enough Attention to the Limitation of Liability Clause?

Parties who seek to allocate risk to the other party often add language meant to underscore the limitation of liability clause. The party will tack on extra language to use as support, should the counterparty claim foul when it realizes, often in hindsight, it cannot recover certain losses following a breach. For example, a party may insert language that the limitation of liability clause is an *"ESSENTIAL ELEMENT"* of the agreement between the parties. A party may assert that it would not have executed the deal without the limitation of liability clause. Further, a party may include language stating certain damages are waived regardless of whether the parties had discussed them beforehand or whether the damages were foreseeable or known to the breaching party. Such language can say the following:

> THE LIMITATIONS OF LIABILITY APPLIES EVEN IF THE BREACHING PARTY HAS BEEN ADVISED OF THE POSSIBILITY OF SUCH DAMAGES IN ADVANCE.

The point of all of these language additions is not to stuff more legalese to an already lengthy provision. Rather, it is to make the parties' agreement on shifting risk and liability exposures abundantly clear and conspicuous. The language is meant to bolster the likelihood that the limitations of liability will apply and be upheld by a court. The party is essentially saying: "Let me spell it out for you once again. You are waiving the right to recover certain damages in the event of a breach, and this could cost you, not me, a substantial sum of money."

If it seems harsh, it is. The bottom line is that you do not want to gloss over the details of a limitation of liability clause. Rather, you want to read those exclusions thoroughly to make sure you understand what the other party will not pay for should it breach the agreement. If you are unclear about what is excluded from recovery, engage in discussions to ensure you are on the same page regarding losses paid in case of a breach.

A simple exercise for you to do beforehand is to brainstorm what could possibly go wrong and list the losses you would suffer if the other party fails to perform or commits wrongdoing. This will prepare you for the discussion on which damages should be recoverable. It can also help you decide whether you really want to provide a blanket waiver of consequential damages. If the types of damages you are most concerned with are expressly listed in a limitation of liability clause, think twice before forfeiting the ability to recover such damages.

With that said, given that most limitation of liability clauses are, and perhaps should be, two-way streets, you have to consider what amount you would pay if you breach the agreement. Try not to lose sight of the damages that you could cause if you fail to perform the contract. You don't want to find yourself facing more liability than you thought you bargained for when you signed the agreement.

Be Prepared to Roll up Your Sleeves

Negotiating a limitation of liability clause is never easy. Practically speaking, most sellers or service providers will give strong push back on modifying a limitation of liability clause. Lawyers consider it one of the most critical legal provisions in a commercial contract for the obvious reason that it limits exposures and potential pay out of significant losses. Therefore, get ready for a protracted back-and-forth negotiation.

It can often be frustrating for a buyer who is faced with a supplier's standard one-sided template agreement. The supplier may promise that the product is safe, will work perfectly, and will not cause any liabilities. "Don't worry, everything will be fine." Yet in the next breath, the supplier will insist on limiting its exposures and capping its liabilities—not really backing up its statements. Ultimately, what parties finally agree to will come down to the party's bargaining positions (who has more leverage) and each party's risk tolerance. Nonetheless, don't be duped into thinking you have nothing to lose after signing off on a limitation of liability clause that waives much of your recovery following a breach.

The Point:

- Knowing what damages you cannot recover from given the limitation of liability clause helps you better understand your exposures should your counterparty breach the agreement.

- Direct damages are essentially damages that one would reasonably expect to arise from a party breaching the agreement and are not typically covered in a limitation of liability clause. You are pretty much in good shape to recover direct damages.

- Consequential, indirect or special damages are best understood as damages that are a consequence of the breach and therefore more removed. They are losses which arise from the special circumstances of the non-breaching party. However, when applied in practice, what constitutes consequential damages can be unclear, depending on the facts and circumstances.

- Sellers or service providers typically set forth in a limitation of liability clause that consequential damages are not recoverable to avoid being exposed to additional risk. But, buyers should be wary. This can cause a dispute later on or leave the buyer unpleasantly surprised and without adequate recovery.

Part II: The Capped Amount

The second part of a limitation of liability clause typically addresses the amount that a party desires to cap its liability for recoverable damages in case of a breach. For example, a party probably does not want to enter into a contract worth $500 and leave itself exposed to millions of dollars of damages. To that end, it is commonplace to find a cap, or maximum amount, based on a dollar amount or a proscribed formula, a party agrees to be exposed to in case of a breach.

A typical mutual template provision may look like this:

TO THE MAXIMUM EXTENT PERMITTED BY LAW, NEITHER PARTY'S LIABILITY FOR ANY CLAIM ARISING UNDER THIS AGREEMENT WILL EXCEED THE TOTAL AMOUNT PAID BY A PARTY UNDER THIS AGREEMENT DURING THE TWELVE MONTHS PRIOR TO THE EVENT GIVING RISE TO THE LIABILITY.

The purpose of the above provision is to make sure the parties' relationship does not create liabilities that exceed the value of the contract. The parties are essentially seeking to limit their risk commensurate to the size of the deal. This may or may not be satisfactory to you. When you break down the above language, it limits the amount of liability twofold: (1) by the amount actually "paid" and (2) to the "twelve-months prior to the event giving rise to the liability." In effect, should the relationship turn sour, you are essentially left with, at most, a possible twelve-month refund. And if the breach happens in the first month into the agreement, the amount is substantially smaller. It doesn't feel as though the other party is risking much.

Should you come across a provision similar to the above, decide whether this liability amount is enough to cover you if your counterparty breaches the agreement. You want to carefully consider the amount you will be comfortable with limiting the liability exposure. Once you figure out the amount, you can seek to modify the above language if necessary.

Keep in mind the party that is more exposed frequently starts with, at least on the first draft, a one-sided, low or ambiguous damages cap. The other party will be tasked with fairly allocating the risk between the parties to the contract. For example, if you are the other party, you can modify the language to give yourself more protection by stating the damages amount will not exceed:

THE GREATER OF (I) TWO TIMES THE TOTAL AMOUNT PAID OR PAYABLE UNDER THIS AGREEMENT OR (II) FIFTY-THOUSAND DOLLARS ($50,000).

The above example does three things. First, you are increasing the liability amount to include the total amount due or "payable" under the contract, not just the amount paid to date. In other words, when a breach occurs you are not stuck calculating what you have already "paid" to the other party to figure out your potential recovery. In reality, such language is not logical, as the potential risks may not correlate to the amounts already paid under an agreement. What if you have not paid anything yet? Instead, you can expand the potential liability for the counterparty to the total amount "payable" under the agreement so the full contract value is taken into account.

Second, while it is common to include language that states liability is capped to the amount "paid twelve (12) months prior to the event giving rise to the liability", the newly crafted example deletes such language. Practically speaking, what if an expensive liability arises three months into the contract. Why should that severely limit damages you can recover? The costs and liabilities could far exceed the amount paid during those initial three months. The above seeks to cap damages on the basis of the aggregate contract price as opposed to the fees paid over a particular time period. This may not be agreeable to the other side, though. If you are entering into a long-term contract, a party may want to specify a time period, such as twelve (12) months, for the calculation to be based on an annual amount.

Regardless of the form, don't lose sight of the fact that the value of the contract (or amount paid or payable under the contract) may not match the value of the risk assumed by a party. In reality, the amount of fees paid or payable may have no bearing on the degree of risk in the contract. For example, you can hire a company for $10,000 to securely store consumer data, yet that company can recklessly allow a data breach and now you are left with millions in damages. You may have to pay to comply with government investigations, notify affected individuals, deal with substantial reputational harm and potentially defend multiple lawsuits, including class action litigation brought by consumers impacted by the data breach. Thus, before agreeing to any liability cap, think through actual losses that could arise should a worst-case scenario occur. If the losses are greater than the price of the contract, make sure to negotiate a higher cap. Simply adding a multiple to the formula (as set forth above) can do wonders to provide additional coverage for worst-case scenarios.

Third, the above example provides a cleaner method of determining liabilities by outlining an actual dollar amount. For practical reasons, if the circumstances allow, it may be preferable to include a reasonable fixed dollar cap in a limitation of liability clause. It provides more certainty to both parties involved. One party knows the maximum potential liability it may face with respect to particular exposures, while the other party knows the maximum potential recovery for losses suffered in relation to a particular risk. Moreover, including a "greater of" technique can be beneficial. Such ensures the damages cap is not tied solely to fees, which can be unreasonably low compared to damages incurred.

However, keep in mind that if you insist on greater coverage, the other party may counter with an increase in price. In some cases, pricing can be tied to risk allocation. As the risk for your counterparty increases, be prepared for the counterparty to demand that pricing be revisited to cover any additional risk.

Finally, it is necessary to point out that there are no guarantees that a court will enforce a limitation of liability clause. If a limitation of liability clause is egregious or so one-sided that it is unreasonable under the circumstances, it is possible that a court will invalidate such a clause. Thus, if a party caps its limitation of liability amount at $20, and the damages are in the tens of thousands, there is a good chance a court will invalidate the clause as unfair (or as we say in the legal world, "unconscionable"). Courts have held that limitation of liability clauses are unenforceable if the contract was not freely negotiated between parties or void against public policy (*i.e.*, the court felt the parties had unequal bargaining power and the clause was woefully unfair). Thus, forcing a limitation of liability clause on a party and providing no room for negotiation can lead to the opposing party challenging it before a court. So, don't be too greedy.

With that said, generally speaking, if the limitation of liability clause is entered into between sophisticated parties, or parties of relatively equal bargaining strength, and is reasonable and clearly drafted, it will likely be enforceable and validated. Courts are not in the practice of saving you from your missteps of failing to negotiate a more balanced limitation of liability clause. Rather, it is up to you to protect yourself.

The Point:

- Whichever side of the bargaining table you are on, the key is to figure out the liability amount you are comfortable accepting before agreeing to any cap on potential recovery.

- Think about what could potentially go wrong as a result of the product or service. How likely it is to occur? If it does occur, what impact will it have on you? Assume the worst when making that analysis.

- Once you decide on the amount and whether you will agree to a cap, carefully read the limitation of liability clause to confirm it clearly reflects your understanding, and that the cap is sufficient to cover potential losses. Do not leave yourself exposed to unwanted risks.

- Don't forget that a limitation of liability clause can be challenged in the courts as unenforceable if the clause is not clear and conspicuous (hence the ALL CAPS) and the non-beaching party lacked power or sophistication to freely negotiate the clause.

What to Watch Out for in a Limitation of Liability Clause

Not Mutual

Always check to make sure the limitation of liability clause is not one-sided and that your exposures are also limited under the clause. You will be better off if restrictions on paying out damages apply to you too. That way, you have reciprocity. Should you breach the contract, you also have rights that limit your liability to the counterparty. You certainly don't want your liability to be unlimited while your counterparty's is capped. Seems unfair.

Often times, a party will take the easy route and simply make the party language mutual. For example, this can be done by changing the language so it states in the consequential damages disclaimer: *"NEITHER PARTY SHALL BE LIABLE TO THE OTHER PARTY FOR . . . "* You also want to modify the damages cap, providing that in no event shall EITHER PARTY'S aggregate liability exceed the amount described. This is not to say it is always the case that you can make these simple mark-ups and be all set, but it is a common legal technique.

Excluding Direct Damages

If a limitation of liability clause sneaks in the word "DIRECT" damages, seeking to waive your recovery of direct damages, cross it out. Such language is hardly standard. Let's put it this way: As discussed above, there are primarily only direct damages and indirect damages (also referred to as special or consequential damages) you can receive in a breach. So, if you exclude them both, in theory, you can recover nothing. It really does not make much sense for a limitation of liability clause to exclude anything other than indirect damages. Unless you feel comfortable going unpaid should a breach occur, closely evaluate a consequential damages disclaimer that includes a "DIRECT" damages exclusion. At a minimum, question the other party on that one.

Don't Let These Limits Apply to Indemnity Costs

One of the trickiest parts of a limitation of liability clause can be understanding whether it is meant to also apply to indemnification liabilities. The details of an indemnification clause, which essentially provides that a party will defend and pay for a third-party lawsuit arising from its performance (or non-performance) of the contract, is set forth later in this book. What is important is that you recognize whether the contract clearly distinguishes between indemnity obligations owed to third parties and limitations of liabilities for damages between parties.

A limitation of liability clause can be drafted so broadly that it will be interpreted as an overall liability cap on the whole contract. It may be your understanding at the time of the agreement that this provision was meant only for liabilities that can occur between the parties and not a third-party indemnity claim. You may be thinking that indemnification is separate and is set forth in a different provision elsewhere in the agreement. But BEWARE, this can be a mistake. A GIGANTIC mistake.

Without appropriate language that expressly states in the beginning of a limitation of liability clause—"EXCEPT FOR A PARTY'S INDEMNIFICATION OBLIGATIONS HEREUNDER"—your counterparty can argue the limitation of liability clause was meant to exclude consequential damages and/or place a cap for all liabilities, including indemnity liabilities owed under the agreement. If an agreement contains both limitation of liability and indemnification clauses, parties must negotiate whether to carve out indemnification liabilities from the limitation of liability clause.

This is a crucial point not to be missed. If you do not make clear that a limitation of liability clause does *not* apply to indemnity obligations, you can be unintentionally and severely limiting your indemnity recovery. You can be left paying money out of pocket when a third party sues you because of your counterparty's mistakes. For this reason, it is preferable to be abundantly clear by expressly stating the limitation of liability clause excludes the indemnification obligations of parties (presuming that is what both parties desire).

In other words, you are ensuring indemnity obligations are separate and uncapped. They are not subject to the restrictions on recoverable losses in a limitation of liability clause. You are essentially telling the other party: "You need to bear full responsibility for any harm you cause to third parties."

Another way to make that point is to provide language at the end of the limitation of liability clause that states:

NOTWITHSTANDING THE FOREGOING, THIS LIMITATION OF LIABILITY CLAUSE DOES NOT APPLY TO A PARTY'S INDEMNIFICATION OBLIGATIONS SET FORTH IN SECTION [X].

Other Common Carve-Outs in a Limitation of Liability Clause

Certain missteps are just too serious to allow the other party to avoid paying for losses. The below sets forth particular breaches that could bring about large exposures and can be carved out of (or not affected by) a limitation of liability clause.

Confidentiality and Security Breaches

If the risk is too great, parties may agree to exclude confidentiality or security breaches in a limitation of liability clause. As a purchaser of a product or service, you may be handing over sensitive information that could have serious and costly consequences if publicly disclosed. Remember, a $10,000 contract for securing data could lead to a $10,000,000 liability should there be an unauthorized disclosure. Given this reality, you may seek to add the following language:

THE LIMITATION OF LIABILITY CLAUSE SHALL NOT APPLY TO DAMAGES CAUSED BY A PARTY'S BREACH OF ITS OBLIGATIONS OF CONFIDENTIALITY AND SECURITY UNDER THE AGREEMENT.

Alternatively, if your counterparty will not agree to exclude entirely these types of damages from a limitation of liability clause, you can negotiate a higher cap to apply for these types of damages. In other words, you can insist on a separate clause that addresses these more serious breaches and provides additional coverage to recoup losses.

Negligence and Misconduct

Also common is to protect yourself from your counterparty being "negligent" or engaging in "misconduct." If the counterparty is negligent (*i.e.*, careless), you probably do not want it to fall back on its limitation of liability clause. Rather, you will prefer it pays for the mess it made. To that point, you can add language like this:

THE LIMITATION OF LIABILITY CLAUSE SHALL NOT APPLY TO DAMAGES CAUSED BY A PARTY'S NEGLIGENCE OR MISCONDUCT.

But, your counterparty can push back on this carve out as the exposure may be too much. Expect your counterparty, at a minimum, to insist on raising the bar by requiring a royal screw up for it to face unlimited liability. This can be accomplished by modifying the above language to say "*gross* negligence," "fraudulent acts," or "*willful* misconduct." If your counterparty insists on such a change, consider defining those terms to reduce uncertainty and confusion later on, as it may not be apparent what actions would fall within such a carve out. As further discussed in the indemnification section, what ultimately constitutes as "gross negligence," as opposed to ordinary negligence, can often be unclear and set a higher than anticipated threshold. Also, practically speaking, keep in mind, if a party actually engages in willful misconduct or fraudulent acts, a court may not enforce the limitation of liability clause and allow for full recovery of losses.

Infringement of Intellectual Property

While not as common, a party can insist that it is not appropriate to limit liability for infringement of intellectual property. A party may not want to assume any liability if the counterparty's product turns out to infringe on another's rights. Practically, however, the counterparty who is seeking to minimize risk exposures will likely push back on such exclusion. No need to fret. If you are covered with appropriate indemnification protections for intellectual property claims (and that indemnification is carved out from the limitation of liability), you will have coverage from third-party lawsuits, which are often the largest liability exposures.

Have You Considered Insurance Coverage?

If parties are concerned about managing risks borne by each party, they can explore obtaining insurance to cover future liabilities. That way, both parties can increase the cap in a limitation of liability clause (or an indemnity clause) to account for insurance coverage to pay for potential claims. Depending on the industry, insurance clauses can be commonplace and useful to protect against losses and substantial exposures. In business contracts, a party can request different types of insurance, such as, but not limited to, commercial general liability coverage, business automobile liability coverage, workers' compensation coverage, technology errors and omissions coverage (for cybersecurity claims), and/or umbrella/excess liability coverage.

However, before you agree with your counterparty to provide insurance, make sure you actually have the types of insurance being requested, as well as minimum coverage amounts. Often times, it is worth a quick email to your insurance broker with the contractual language. The broker likely receives requests like these on a routine basis. Also, don't forget to ask yourself whether the insurance amounts are in fact sufficient for the risks associated with the contract. You want to make sure any policy limits are enough to absorb the potential liability exposure.

Furthermore, keep in mind, simply requiring a party to have liability insurance only provides coverage to that party; there may be no insurance coverage under said policy for you, unless you specifically ask and confirm you are named as an "additional insured" under the policy. Moreover, if the counterparty is seeking to be named on the insurance policy as an "additional insured", you will want to contact your insurance provider to confirm this is doable.

Lastly, it goes without saying that it is wise not to agree to providing insurance you do not maintain or cannot provide. Likewise, do not agree to add a counterparty as an additional insured if you have no intention of actually doing so. While these practical tips may sound silly, you would be amazed how many companies agree to insurance clauses without checking whether they actually have the insurance they agreed to maintain.

The Point:

- A liability cap could be favorable if it is: (i) reasonable in the amount depending on the circumstances, (ii) applies to both parties (if mutuality makes sense); and (iii) excludes liabilities that should not be limited.

- Double check that indemnification obligations are expressly carved out of a limitation of liability clause if you don't want to restrict your indemnity recovery. Also pay close attention to any other carve outs, which can result in an uncapped liability exposure.

- Consider whether the parties should explore negotiating an insurance provision to help pay for any liability claim and alleviate risk exposure.

Should You Agree on a Liquidated Damages Clause?

What if the parties don't want to rely entirely on a limitation of liability clause, and would rather agree in advance to the amount of damages owed following a breach? Parties may desire to establish a predetermined, fixed sum of money that must be paid upon the occurrence of a specific event, such as if the other party fails to perform as promised. In other words, parties may agree upfront to monetary damages owed in case things fall apart. This type of provision is known as a "liquidated damages clause." Unlike a limitation of liability clause, where parties cap liability or exclude recovery of certain losses, parties set a specific dollar amount to be paid if a particular event (such as a breach) occurs.

Often times, such a clause is utilized when injury from a breach of contract may be uncertain or difficult to quantify. For example, how do you measure "reputational damages" if a breach causes a party reputational harm? The practical answer is that it is difficult and, in litigation, would take experts and expensive discovery. In light of this, parties may consider agreeing on a dollar amount to avoid a dispute over damages altogether. In theory, the dollar amount is meant to function so a party facing a breach can recover a reasonable amount of estimated losses. The amount payable under a liquidated damages clause should be a genuine estimate of the loss to be suffered by the non-breaching party. It must be reasonable and proportionate to the anticipated harm and should not act as a penalty for a breach.

With that said, in practice, a contract may include a liquidated damages provision that seeks a pay out of an unreasonable amount. A party may have boilerplate language that inserts an unusually high amount in case of a breach. Instead of seeking an amount reasonable in light of anticipated or likely harm for a breach, a party may fix an excessive amount to act as a deterrent or a punishment. This is not, however, the intent of a liquidated damages clause. Again, the clause is not meant to be penal in nature. Rather, the predetermined amount is supposed to be a genuine, good faith estimate of the extent of loss suffered in case of a breach.

A bare-bones liquidated damages clause may look like this:

If Seller breaches its obligation to deliver goods in accordance with the terms and conditions in this contract, Buyer shall recover $X as liquidated damages. The Parties stipulate that the agreed upon sum is not a penalty.

Legally, a court would likely void a liquidated damages clause that includes an inflated dollar amount disproportionate to actual harm suffered. A liquidated damages provision is typically only enforceable if: (i) the injury is uncertain or difficult to quantify; (ii) the stated amount is reasonable and proportionate to the harm suffered under the circumstances and (iii) the clause does not function as a penalty. You are essentially inviting litigation if you agree to an unreasonable liquidated damages clause and there is a breach down the road.

Thus, a party is better off negotiating an appropriate liquidated damages provision or not agreeing to one in the first place. For example, a party may seek to negotiate any such clause down to provide payment for actual costs only or incurred expenses. That way, a party is not paying for an amount above and beyond the loss actually suffered. Alternatively, a party may choose to cross out a liquidated damages clause altogether, finding it inappropriate to agree ahead of time on a pre-determined fixed damages amount.

The Point:

- Keep an eye out for a liquidated damages clause that fixes an unusually high dollar amount to compensate for a breach. Such essentially invites litigation and is not good for anyone involved, as the breaching party will likely dispute the clause and refuse to pay the stated amount.

- While a liquidated damages provision is not supposed to function as a penalty, in practice, it can come across as such. Thus, think carefully before you agree to pay out a predetermined sum of money for a breach.

Representations and Warranties

Depending on the nature of the relationship, a party may provide certain affirmative statements of fact, which the other party will rely upon, in entering into the business contract. These statements about factual matters are referred to in a contract as "representations" and "warranties", which set forth express assurances that parties are making to each other. It is as if parties are saying to one another: "If what you are saying is true, then stand by your word and put in writing that you attest such is in fact true today and will be true later on."

Technically speaking, the terms "representations" and "warranty" are not synonymous and have different meanings and applications under the law. Each gives rise to a different legal remedy if the relationship turns sour and parties end up fighting in court. From a practical perspective, however, the difference between these terms does not really matter, as they are commonly lumped together in commercial contracts. In practice, the terms "representations" and "warranties" are often combined together and treated interchangeably, with language such as: *"Each Party represents and warrants to the other Party X, Y, Z."*

Parties to a business contract typically represent and warrant a variety of statements of fact. There is no one-size-fits-all standardized language for a representations and warranties clause. This is because such clauses are tailored to the particular parties' agreement and goods and services provided. What a party will represent and warrant will vary from contract to contract. Most important, if a party tells you something and you rely on that representation when deciding to enter into the business relationship, include it in the contract. Failure to do so can leave you empty handed.

For example, to the extent a party is providing you a license to use intellectual property (such as a photograph), you may require a representation and warranty that the supplier has rights to supply such license. When the party is representing that it has the rights to supply you the photograph, hold that party to its word and include it in the contract. Specifically, the supplier may provide a broad representation and warranty that *"it has the full right to license all intellectual property rights that it licences to the other Party under the Agreement."*

If, for example, a party supplies a product, such as a contract for software, a customer may request a warranty that the software conforms with agreed upon specifications and is free from viruses. Another perhaps more relatable example is that of purchasing a car. You may insist the car salesperson represents and warrants that the car is, and will be, free from certain defects for a period of time or that the selling company has title to the car. No one wants to purchase a car only to discover later it has a faulty engine or the seller did not actually own the car.

Furthermore, a service provider may warrant to a consumer that it will perform services with reasonable care and skill and in accordance with generally recognized commercial practices and standards. In other words, the supplier may warrant that it will provide services as promised, and if it does not, the consumer can sue for breach. Ultimately, whatever representations and warranties, if any, parties agree upon depend on the nature of the relationship, the statements of fact that are made during negotiations, and the goods and services supplied.

Although the clause is often tailored to particular circumstances of the parties, there are a few representations and warranties customarily found in business contracts. For example, many business contracts set forth that a party represents and warrants it has authority to execute the agreement and will comply with applicable laws when performing under the agreement. In theory, without a representation and warranty stating the party will comply with applicable laws, it could violate laws and the other party may not have language to point to for claiming breach. Practically speaking, it can be difficult to disagree with the other party when it wants you to confirm you will not violate the law. Try saying out loud: "No, I will not agree to that as I cannot promise to comply with the law."

A representations and warranties clause in a business contract can look like this:

> *Each Party represents and warrants to the other Party that: (i) it has full power and authority to execute and deliver this Agreement and to comply with the provisions of, and perform all its obligations and exercise all of its rights under, this Agreement; (ii) all consents, licenses, approvals and authorizations required in connection with the entry into, performance, validity and enforceability of this Agreement have been obtained and are in full force and effect; (iii) it has the full right to license any*

intellectual property rights that it licenses to the other Party under this Agreement; and (iv) it will comply with all applicable laws, rules and regulations in respect of the performance of its obligations and exercise of its rights under this Agreement.

The Point:

- When you review a representations and warranties clause, confirm you are comfortable with what the other party is providing as assurances, as well as what you are providing as assurances.

- If there is a crucial fact or circumstance that needs to remain true for the relationship to be successful, it may be appropriate to include it in a representation and warranty.

- At a minimum, consider including representations and warranties that your counterparty has authority to execute and deliver on the agreed upon terms and will comply with applicable laws.

What to Watch Out for in a Representations and Warranties Clause

Representations and Warranties Tied to an Indemnification Clause

If a party's representation turns out to be false or if it breaches a warranty, this can cause harm, not only to the counterparty, but potentially to a third party. For example, if the supplier did not have any rights to the photo it licensed to you, such could cause damages to you. You may also be sued by the third party who has rights over the photo. Thus, you are now facing both your own losses as well as liabilities stemming from third-party claims. To protect a party from this type of situation, the representations and warranties provided under the agreement are often tied to the indemnification clause. As discussed more fully in the indemnification section of this book, an indemnification provision commonly provides that a party will indemnify the other party for *"any breach by a Party of any representation, covenant, warranty, provision or obligation under the Agreement."* Therefore, if a party fails to comply with a representation and warranty, such party will be exposing itself to an indemnity claim.

In practice, this is standard and often reasonable. Think of it this way: If a supplier's assurances about its products or services turns out to be false, and this results in a third-party claim, you would expect the buyer to demand the supplier pay for such third-party lawsuit. In essence, if a supplier does not stand by its word and causes harm to a third party, you can bet the buyer will not be pleased and will seek indemnity. On the other hand, if you are the seller providing representations and warranties, understand whether your assurances made in the agreement are tied to the indemnification clause and consider your exposures. A supplier does not want to give a representation and warranty that is untrue, or that could become untrue later on, as the liability risk can be costly. By limiting representation and warranty language, a supplier can also limit the scope of its indemnity obligation if the clauses are linked together, which is often the case.

No Ability to Terminate if Breached Warranty

If a party provides you a warranty promising the product will work for a particular purpose and such turns out to be untrue, you may be entitled to damages. You can seek to claim for losses incurred as a result of the breach of warranty. However, depending on how the contract was drafted, you may have no right to actually terminate for a breach of warranty. Thus, you could be stuck with a product that is not satisfying your expectations and no ability to exit the agreement. For this reason, having a termination "for convenience" clause, as discussed earlier, allowing you to terminate for any reason whatsoever can solve this problem. Also, negotiating a means to terminate if a representation or warranty is breached is another alternative. With the ability to terminate, you are not stuck and can remove yourself from a bad situation, or at least use such provision as leverage, should promises made by the other party turn out to be untrue.

Warranty Disclaimers

Take notice of language that disclaims warranties. To understand why business contracts contain disclaimer language, you have to understand a few basic legal principles. Generally speaking, the law can automatically include certain "implied" warranties in a commercial contract even if they are not written down. Given this, it is commonplace for a supplier to have a section expressly disclaiming those warranties so as to avoid a court implying assurances in the agreement.

In order to disclaim warranties to the maximum extent permitted under the law, a supplier may include language stating the product or service is provided "as is." This essentially means the supplier is not providing you any assurances. In other words, "you get what you get." A broad, blanket warranty disclaimer language, seeking to disclaim any and all implied warranties as allowed under the law will generally stand out in the contract. This is because certain laws require a disclaimer of warranties to be conspicuous. Such a clause can, for example, be in ALL CAPS, and look like this:

ANY PRODUCTS AND SERVICES OFFERED BY PARTY ARE PROVIDED "AS IS." NEITHER PARTY NOR ANY OF PARTY'S AFFILIATES MAKES ANY REPRESENTATION OR WARRANTY OF ANY KIND, WHETHER EXPRESS, IMPLIED, STATUTORY,

OR OTHERWISE WITH RESPECT TO THE SERVICE OR PRODUCT OFFERINGS, EXCEPT TO THE EXTENT PROHIBITED BY APPLICABLE LAW. PARTY AND ITS AFFILIATES AND LICENSORS DISCLAIM ALL WARRANTIES WITH RESPECT TO THE PRODUCTS, INCLUDING ANY IMPLIED WARRANTIES OF MERCHANTABILITY, SATISFACTORY QUALITY, FITNESS FOR A PARTICULAR PURPOSE, NON-INFRINGEMENT, AND QUIET ENJOYMENT, AND ANY WARRANTIES ARISING OUT OF ANY COURSE OF DEALING, PERFORMANCE, OR TRADE USAGE.

Beware if you agree to language like the above and a problem arises with the product or service. You can be sure your counterparty will point to the disclaimer to avoid legal responsibility if things get sticky. With that said, you also cannot lose sight that this would be terrible business practice if the product or service fails and the supplier responds with: "I never assured you our product would work for you."

In practice, parties may work out any warranty issues in order to maintain a positive business relationship. Often times, when there is a warranty issue, both sides have incentives to work out a commercial resolution and continue with the contract. Otherwise, the seller will likely lose all future business and possibly face reputational harm should word get out about the poor product. Nonetheless, if you are a buyer, and you have bargaining leverage, consider pushing back on the supplier if it fails to provide you adequate warranties. This is especially so if you are purchasing a good or service that needs to work for a particular purpose and you have communicated such to the supplier. As a buyer, having representations and warranties will give you comfort and language to point to should the product or service not work to your expectations.

Indemnification

The indemnification clause in a contract is arguably an attorney's biggest worry of potential exposure in a business relationship. It is perhaps the most negotiated provision in a commercial agreement. At its most basic level, the purpose of an indemnification clause is to transfer the risk of loss and liabilities from one party to another. Attorneys often go to this clause first in an agreement and mark it up. This clause also requires the most explanation to business colleagues so they truly understand the real risk and liability exposure an indemnification clause can bring to the company.

Under a standard indemnification clause, each party agrees to *"indemnify, defend and hold harmless"* the other party should its actions cause a third-party claim to surface. In effect, the premise of an indemnification clause is: "I am in a business relationship with you and if you do something that causes a third-party to sue me, I want you to take care of it for me." In other words, if you cause harm to a third-party, *indemnify* me by paying for it: "I want you to have my back." You are also saying *defend* me against a third-party claim: "pay for my large legal bills should I get sued because you caused an expensive third-party lawsuit." In practice, most consider the term *hold harmless* to be synonymous with the word indemnify.

Let's look at an example of how this can play out in practice. What if you purchase a photograph from a merchant for $50? Then, months later, you are served with a legal notice. You find out a photographer is suing you, claiming he has rights to the photo, and is seeking $10,000 in damages. The photographer could be lying and he may not have even taken the picture, but this does not matter to you. Third parties can sue for many reasons and often claims have no merit but are—without a doubt—costly to defend. Indeed, in such a circumstance, you may be forced to retain an attorney to defend a copyright lawsuit, who could conceivably cost more than the $10,000 in damages the photographer is demanding. You are now in an expensive situation, and all of this for a $50 photograph.

Sounds scary, because it is. This is why attorneys focus on the indemnification provision perhaps the most of any part of the business contract. But, no need to be concerned. Simply understand how to protect yourself with an indemnification clause and your exposures will be limited. Well, at least the counterparty will be paying for your lawyers and dealing with this claim—not you.

The indemnification clause may look complicated at first glance, since it contains a bunch of legal language. However, it is not difficult to understand once you break it down. Indeed, most indemnification clauses follow the same structure and look redundant when you understand the basic language employed in this type of clause.

One practical rule of thumb is to ask the following: Do you have the ability to recover for losses you could incur from costly third-party lawsuits, and get out of the contract if needed? If you have no time to review an agreement or have fifteen minutes of free legal counsel, at a minimum, ask for two things: (1) your indemnification clause properly covers you and does not expose you to unreasonable risk and (2) you have a termination for convenience clause so you can exit the relationship if necessary.

Getting to the Bottom of an Indemnification Clause

An indemnification clause typically has three parts, which are often written in the following order:

The Who: Who are the parties covered that could be sued by a third party. This is where you list the players whom a third party could potentially sue if something goes wrong. It is the parties and those related to them that can be injured or named in a lawsuit, should the counterparty commit wrongdoing under the agreement. You typically see players listed, such as: your company and its affiliates, and each of their respective officers, directors, employees, representatives and agents. The clause may also go further and list subsidiaries, parent companies, stockholders and permitted successors and assigns. Not as common, though, is a party inserting the term ''customers,'' which can be overreaching and increase exposures beyond what is appropriate. Beware of this practice, as you may not want to indemnify the other party's customers should you mess up.

The "Who" essentially means if a claim is asserted against any of these entities or people, such parties can potentially seek reimbursement from the indemnifying party under the agreement. You can always consider narrowing the definition, *i.e.*, crossing out those in the list who should not be considered indemnified parties.

The What: What exactly is the counterparty agreeing to cover? This is where a party lists what types of liabilities and losses the counterparty is willing to take responsibility for and foot the bill. What you typically find in an agreement is VERY broad language stating that the counterparty is responsible for: all actions, causes of actions, suits, claims, demands, complaints, investigations, liabilities, losses, costs, judgments, damages and fees and expenses (including reasonable attorney's fees and amounts paid in settlement).

As the indemnified party, the broader you make this list, the more you are protected. For sure, you want to expressly state that attorney's fees would be covered; however most qualify the language limiting recovery of only "reasonable" attorney's fees. That said, retaining an attorney and paying for legal fees and costs will be your first headache when a third party threatens you for something your counterparty did wrong. Having an indemnification clause that pays for the bills and/or retains the attorney on your behalf is key.

The Which: Which type of claims and events are covered? Now this is the trickiest part of the indemnification provision and the most negotiated. The "Who" and the "What" are pretty straightforward and can feel boilerplate. Deciding "Which" events are covered can lead to more difficult conversations. This part of an indemnification clause essentially sets forth risks the indemnifying party could cause that would result in liability. There are essentially two main formats that you can negotiate.

The Broad: Cover It All. While this is less common, you can agree that any third-party claim arising from the counterparty's performance of the contract, or from its products or services, is covered under the indemnification provision. With a broad indemnity, the counterparty can be obligated to pay for, and defend against, any type of third-party lawsuit (or a mere threatened claim) relating to its conduct. Below is an example of a broad indemnification clause:

> *Party will indemnify, defend and hold harmless the other Party and its affiliates, and each of their respective officers, directors, employees, representatives and agents (each an "Indemnified Party"), from and against any and all actions, causes of actions, claims, demands, liabilities, losses, costs, damages and fees and expenses (including reasonable attorney's fees and amounts paid in settlement) (collectively, "Claim" or "Claims") which an Indemnified Party may at any time incur, sustain or*

become subject to by reason of any Claim brought, asserted or alleged, by a third party arising out of or related in any way to any services provided by or obtained through Party or the Party's performance of the Agreement.

The broader the indemnity language, the greater the indemnifying party's exposure and liability. An overly broad indemnification clause may force the indemnifying party to assume a wide variety of risks. Thus, you will want to weigh which party is more likely to be indemnifying the other before agreeing to one way or another. The party with the greater risk will be less likely to agree on such broad coverage, as it can provide too much exposure for potentially large and unpredictable losses. Keep in mind that a requirement to pay attorney's fees alone can result in astronomical costs for the indemnifying party.

On the flip side, practically speaking, the party exposed to potential third-party claims resulting from the other party's failed performance will want an indemnification provision as broad as possible. Sure, it is rational to want to shift all financial liability from third-party claims to your counterparty. But let's be realistic here. Your counterparty will likely not want to be responsible for every possible claim that could arise from its performance of the contract. So, while you may try to obtain the ultimate management of risk exposures (and, by all means, go for it!), don't be surprised when your counterparty gives push back or disapproves. As a further matter, if the indemnification clause is drafted too broadly, you run the risk of a court choosing not to enforce the indemnity at all.

The Limited: Crafting a Customized List. If a party does not want to be responsible for every claim that could arise due to its performance under the agreement, it will put forth a list of categories of claims it feels comfortable indemnifying the other party. This is the more common route in a business contract. In theory, the list should be tailored to the most relevant exposures that could arise due to the business relationship and should be reasonable under the circumstances. In practice, you cannot rely on your counterparty to draft a fair and balanced indemnification clause. Parties are often left to fend for themselves and to negotiate and craft the exposures they want covered under the indemnity.

Let's go back to the picture example. If the counterparty is selling you a photograph, you will want to think what third-party claims could arise from the purchase of the photograph. The obvious risk is that a third party, such as the photographer, could come forward and claim your counterparty did not have the right to sell the photo, so now pay up. Given this risk, you will want to negotiate the indemnification clause to expressly state that the counterparty will indemnify you if a third party claims: "that's my photo." Or, put in legal terms, the third party claims that "you are infringing on my intellectual property rights" and asserts a copyright suit against you.

Put simply, you don't want to pay for a photograph and then be stuck with a lawsuit because your counterparty did not own the photo in the first place. To protect yourself for that risk, you would include language that makes clear the counterparty will pay for any claims the photograph "infringes in any manner on any intellectual property rights (including copyright)."

Below is what the clause would look like. Notice, just the last sentence is modified—the "who" and "what" stayed the same.

> *Party will indemnify, defend and hold harmless the other Party and its affiliates, and each of their respective officers, directors, employees, representatives and agents (each an "Indemnified Party"), from and against any and all actions, causes of*

actions, claims, demands, liabilities, losses, costs, damages and fees and expenses (including reasonable attorney's fees and amounts paid in settlement) (collectively, "Claim" or "Claims") which an Indemnified Party may at any time incur, sustain or become subject to by reason of any Claim brought, asserted or alleged, by a third party that the photographs provided under this Agreement infringe in any manner any intellectual property rights (including copyright).

There are a number of different categories you can list in an indemnification clause to protect yourself from third-party claims. When you review an indemnification clause, ask yourself, "Which risks am I potentially exposed to because I purchased this service or product?" Then check to see if they are covered. In other words, think about the "what ifs" that could occur and draft protections in the agreement to cover your worst-case scenarios.

For example, if the counterparty is providing you software or technology, you may want to be protected if a third party sues you for patent infringement. "I bought your software for $150, now a third party is suing me for $250,000 claiming patent infringement, pay up." If the counterparty has access to any sensitive information, you will want to be protected from unauthorized disclosures. "I provided you confidential data about my customers, and you disclosed it to the public, now my customers are suing me for millions, pay up." If the counterparty is supplying you content (such as photos, video, etc.) you are displaying, you will want to be protected from claims relating to content, such as intellectual property claims. "I purchased a $15,000 video from you to use in my advertisements, now someone is claiming they did not consent to be filmed and is demanding $50,000, pay up." To the extent you want to encompass a broader category of claims, it is common to include language of indemnity for any claims arising from a breach of the agreement.

Ultimately, you will have to understand what risks the counterparty can cause that can lead to a third-party claim, which means, for you, escalating costs and exposure. Below is a list of common categories, as well as draft language, you may find in an indemnification clause that sets forth which claims or events are covered. Remember, you will likely be providing indemnification too. It is often a two-way street. Thus, you want to be careful about overreaching as your counterparty may seek mutuality with respect to indemnity coverage and potential exposures.

Claims Arising from a Party's Breach of Agreement

> any breach by a Party of any representation, covenant, warranty, provision or obligation under the Agreement.

Claims Arising from a Party's Wrongdoing

> a Party's or its employees' negligence, gross negligence, willful misconduct, fraud, or other unlawful act or failure to act by a Party or any of its employees in relation to the services provided under the Agreement.

Confidentiality or Privacy Violations

> a Party's unauthorized disclosure or use of confidential information or personally identifiable information or noncompliance with applicable data privacy laws or data security laws or regulations.

Intellectual Property or Other Violations of Third Party Rights

> any claim or allegation that a Party's content or technology misappropriates or infringes in any manner any intellectual property right (including any patent, trademark, trade secret, copyright, or other intellectual property right).

any claim or allegation that the Party's content contains any material or information that is obscene, defamatory, libelous, slanderous, or violates any rights of any person or entity, including rights of publicity or privacy.

General Violations of the Law

a Party's violation of any applicable law, rule or regulation.

Injury, Death or Property Damage

all damages for bodily injury, including death, or damage to real or tangible personal property.

If any of the above categories are relevant to your circumstances, plug in the language into the "which" portion, or final part, of the indemnification clause. This will provide you protection against third-party claims should your counterparty commit any of the acts listed. You may also want to keep your own checklist of categories handy as it can make the indemnification negotiation faster. Keeping a checklist of potential exposures is good practice so you do not forget a potential third-party risk, leaving you exposed and wishing you could turn-back-the clock.

Common Issues Arising from Negotiating an Indemnification Clause

Negligence vs. Gross Negligence? A common discussion while negotiating an indemnification clause arises when a party wants to limit its indemnity obligations for acts constituting "gross negligence," while the counterparty seeks indemnification for acts of just "negligence." But is there a real difference?

The answer is yes. The term "negligence" is essentially saying the other party has to indemnify you if a third-party claim arises because your counterparty did something carelessly. If you want to get technical, the law refers to "negligence" as a failure to exercise the standard of care a reasonably prudent person would have in a similar situation. In other words, if you can argue your counterparty made a careless mistake, you are on your way to obtaining indemnification for a third-party claim.

Adding the word "grossly" negligent, changes the equation. It provides a higher standard of what must be shown to obtain indemnification. The problem is that "gross" negligence is somewhat ambiguous. Should your counterparty want to weasel out of indemnifying you, it will claim that, while it made an error, it did not rise to the level of being "grossly" negligent.

The other issue is that, unlike the term "negligent," which is consistently applied as above, there is no universal definition of being "grossly negligent." Courts can apply different definitions depending on the circumstances and which state contract laws apply. A court may interpret "grossly negligent" as something similar to a reckless standard or an extreme departure from the standard of care. In fact, many courts apply a high threshold, often making it difficult for a party to prove negligence was "gross." One thing is for certain, you have to go beyond arguing the counterparty was careless, as that would only cover the lower standard of negligence.

What does this all mean? Practically speaking, if you agree to be indemnified when the counterparty is "grossly negligent" and a third-party claim arises, you will need to be prepared for the counterparty to argue it owes you nothing. The counterparty can argue its actions weren't bad enough to rise to the level of "grossly" negligent. Keep in mind, your counterparty already knows this. It perhaps added the word "grossly" during negotiations to provide a level of complexity and an extra argument to potentially avoid its indemnity liability.

Another way to look at it is that your counterparty has weighed the exposures it is willing to assume and is telling you that, unless it does something really bad, it is not interested in footing your legal bills or paying any third-party claims on your behalf. Each business has its own tolerance on risk exposures it is willing to assume in a particular relationship. A party simply may not have the appetite to cover your losses should a third-party lawsuit arise.

With that said, you cannot lose sight of reality. Should your counterparty cause harm and subject you to a third-party claim, it may still indemnify you if it wants to preserve the business relationship. A counterparty may have an argument that it was not "grossly" negligent and owes no indemnity. However, to the extent your counterparty decides to use the argument and refuse to indemnify you, it will inevitably damage the parties' relationship going forward.

The Point:

- There is a real difference, both legally and practically, between "negligent" and "grossly negligent" when negotiating an indemnification clause.

- "Grossly negligent" comes with a level of uncertainty and gives the violating party wiggle room to refuse to indemnify the other party if its actions were merely careless (*i.e.*, not rising above negligence).

- A party may insist on "grossly negligent" language so it reduces its exposures and does not have to pay for large legal bills and eventual judgments should a third-party claim arise when it just made a mistake.

What to Watch Out for in an Indemnification Clause

So now you know the basics of an indemnification clause. But what language do you want to beware of in an indemnification clause? Below are some tricks of the trade.

Not Mutual. A common practice to beware of when reviewing an indemnification clause is that it is only one-sided. You may receive an agreement that has only one party indemnifying the other party and not vice-a-versa. This is called an indemnification provision that is "not mutual" or a "one-way indemnity." Typically, the party who drafts the agreement and sends over its template may have a one-sided indemnification provision, requiring that you indemnify it under the agreement. This can result in nothing for you should the counterparty screw up and you get sued by a third party. If you spot a non-mutual indemnity clause, you will want to add your own indemnity protections.

There are essentially two main ways to deal with this circumstance.

At the outset, modify the first sentence to say: "*Each Party* agrees to indemnify, defend and hold harmless *the other party* and its affiliates, and each of their respective officers, directors, employees, representatives and agents . . . " Some consider this the lazy way, or the simplest way to make an indemnification provision mutual. It can work well if you have a broad indemnification provision whereby you are each indemnifying each other for any acts performed under the agreement. "Hey, if your counterparty is expecting you to indemnify it for everything under the sun, maybe you want to make it mutual and be on the same footing." However, if you are faced with a category-specific indemnification clause, it does not work as well to simply modify the first sentence. Unfortunately, this practice is done by some and it often does not make sense under the circumstances.

For example, let's go back to the photo scenario. The seller of the photo may give you a boilerplate agreement that has a one-sided indemnification clause saying you will indemnify the seller if you are grossly negligent. If you just change the first sentence to say both parties will indemnify each other for gross negligence, this may not cover you for claims brought by the third party photographer making copyright claims. You are better protected if you craft your own indemnification clause, providing for the categories that fit your particularized risks. This brings us to the second way to craft a mutual, and more fair, indemnification clause.

Put some more thought into the "Which" and consider what categories apply to your exposures. Then draft your own separate indemnification clause. You can decide to copy the counterparty's first couple of sentences (the "Who" and the "What"), but replace the counterparty's name as the party providing the indemnification. That way it does not look like you are creating an entirely new provision and are working within the confines of the agreement provided by your counterparty. However, only go that route if you are satisfied with the initial sentences and are sure they provide you enough coverage. Next, consider adding to and modifying the "Which" by inserting particular categories of risk (see list of examples set forth on pages 76–77 above) you want to be indemnified for in the future.

In the end, recognizing that an indemnification clause is not mutual is a good first step. Drafting an indemnification clause that fits your specific needs and addresses your largest exposures is even smarter.

Covering More than Just Claims from Third Parties. In its traditional and basic format, an indemnification clause in a business contract is meant to cover claims brought by *third parties* who were harmed by a contracting party to the agreement. Remember, it is the saying: "I am in a business relationship with you and if you do something that causes a third party to sue me, I want you to take care of it for me." The real premise of an indemnification clause is to protect the indemnified party against third-party lawsuits. An indemnification clause, however, is typically not intended to cover claims or losses incurred between the contracting parties themselves. Instead, any damages recoverable (or not recoverable) for claims between the parties are often dealt with in a limitation of liability clause, a liquidated damages provision, or other provisions elsewhere within the agreement.

Nevertheless, every once in a while a party will slip language in an indemnification clause that broadens it to cover all claims, even those asserted between parties. For example, rather than having a standard indemnity for any claim brought, asserted or alleged, "by a third party," a party can substitute the words with the phrase *"by any person or entity."* Watch out for this. If your intention is for the indemnity clause to address only third-party claims, then say so, and stick with language providing indemnity for claims asserted "by a third party." Let's revisit the broad indemnity clause:

> *Party will indemnify, defend and hold harmless the other Party and its affiliates, and each of their respective officers, directors, employees, representatives and agents (each an "Indemnified Party"), from and against any and all actions, causes of actions, claims, demands, liabilities, losses, costs, damages and fees and expenses (including reasonable attorney's fees and amounts paid in settlement) (collectively, "Claim" or "Claims") which an*

*Indemnified Party may at any time incur, sustain or become subject to by reason of any Claim brought, asserted or alleged, **by a third party** arising out of or related in any way to any services provided by or obtained through Party or the Party's performance of the Agreement.*

By removing the words "by a third party", your counterparty can attempt to use the indemnity provision as a means to collect direct damages (and, perhaps, even attorney's fees) for breach of contract, when such may not have been the intended purpose. Even worse, if the limitation of liability clause expressly excludes indemnity claims (as addressed earlier in the book), the counterparty can argue its recovery is unlimited. The argument would go something like this: "Given your breach of the agreement, you are obligated to indemnify me and pay for my losses and costs, as well as my counsel's fees. Our indemnification clause is unmistakably clear and applies to all claims, including disputes between parties. There is no cap on indemnity claims, so I will be seeking full recoupment of all losses."

Put simply, you may want to avoid extending the indemnification clause to claims between the contracting parties. Pay close attention to ensure the indemnity clause is not missing the words "third party."

Finally Adjudicated Language. Perhaps some of the worst language added to an indemnification clause is when a party says it will indemnify you to the extent that a claim is *"finally adjudged"* by a court, and after appeals are exhausted. You will see a line stuck in the middle of the clause like this: the counterparty will indemnify you if *"a court of competent jurisdiction, in a judgment that has become final and that is no longer subject to appeal or review,"* determines the counterparty is responsible. This line can cause lawyers to do a slow, deliberate eye roll.

Practically speaking, this phrase can make it rare for a party to ever have to pay out on the indemnity. Let's walk through steps that would have to occur before the counterparty would pay an indemnity claim under this scenario. First, a claim would arise because of something the counterparty did, not you. Nonetheless, you are left to deal with a lawsuit. Then, you would have to suffer through the entire lawsuit and wait for a court to render a ruling. The odds of you sticking through an expensive trial caused by someone else's mistake are unlikely. It is more probable you will want to settle the lawsuit early and not wait for the indemnity money.

Furthermore, the indemnification language says a court must issue a final judgment, which can take months or years. But wait, there is more. Even if you stick through the process and wait all this time for a court judgment, you still do not get your indemnity money. Rather, the provision says now appeals have to be exhausted. So, if an appeal is pursued, you are not getting paid so quickly. In the end, the chance of actually sticking through litigation and waiting to be indemnified from your counterparty is slim. In reality, you will likely settle the lawsuit early and be left with no recourse, perhaps having to bear legal costs and the settlement amount. Unless circumstances are such that parties understand indemnification is extremely limited and may take years to pay out, you may want to cross out that language.

Caps on Indemnification. Other common language that can be added to an indemnification clause seeks to limit the payment exposure by adding a cap on the amount that can be paid out. A party essentially includes language that sets a monetary limit to the indemnification obligation. You will see language like this:

Notwithstanding anything to the contrary contained herein, the indemnification liability herein shall not exceed the amount of $50,000.

OR

Notwithstanding anything to the contrary contained herein, the indemnification liability herein shall be limited to twice the amount of the monies paid or payable under the Agreement.

Practically speaking, an indemnity cap may not be a bad idea. For example, if you are the party more likely to cause third-party harm (*i.e.*, you are providing services or products), then you may favor a cap. Similar to a limitations of liability damages cap addressed earlier, an indemnity cap can provide predictability and certainty in managing risk allocation and liability exposures.

Moreover, if parties cannot agree on appropriate indemnification language, with one party wanting to limit the indemnity (maybe even putting in the final adjudication language above) and the other party wanting more protection, discussing a cap is a means towards compromise. Your counterparty may say, "We are not giving you a broad indemnification, it provides too much exposure for us." You can respond, "Well, one idea is that we can agree on a cap for indemnity claims. That way, I make sure I am broadly covered and we have an understanding of the total amount paid should a problem arise."

The risk of going this route is that the cap you negotiate may not cover your losses when a third-party problem arises. Remember, it was likely the other party's wrongdoing that caused the third-party lawsuit, so capping the amount may seem unfair to you. Thus, if you decide to negotiate a capped amount, you have to put thought into what actual exposures could potentially arise and choose an amount that provides you with sufficient protection. You do not want to be footing the bill when the other party caused harm that prompted a third-party claim. When that happens, you will be annoyed you did not negotiate a sufficient cap.

If you agree to a provision stating your counterparty will only pay to indemnify for an amount up to twice, or three times, the amount paid under the agreement, then you are limited by a multiple of what was paid to date. Be careful about a provision that caps indemnity at just the amount you have paid, as then you are basically getting a refund when you have a lawsuit on your hands. Keep in mind, the value of a contract may not necessarily correlate with the harm a party can cause to a third party. It is up to you to decide what amount makes the most sense if you decide to negotiate an indemnity cap.

Furthermore, practically speaking, consider the psychological component of an indemnity cap in a business relationship. Your counterparty may be worried about conceding its indemnification obligation if the liability is uncapped and uncertain. The counterparty may be incentivized to apply a more narrow interpretation of the indemnification clause to avoid unknown exposure. But, if your indemnification liability is capped in clear terms, the counterparty may be less likely to dispute the indemnification clause because it has certainty over the exposure— it knows ahead of time its maximum pay out. Thus, depending on how negotiations unfold, consider exploring an indemnity cap you determine is reasonable under the circumstances. If you cannot get a broad and unlimited indemnity, it can be a good, next-best option to keep in mind.

Indemnification Obligations Surviving Past Termination

Another common practice relating to an indemnification clause is to provide language stating the clause survives termination or expiration of the agreement. This was addressed briefly in the book's survival clause section. The purpose is to prevent a party from attempting to avoid its indemnification obligations by terminating the agreement or arguing the claim was brought after the agreement was terminated or expired. Technically, without language that the indemnification clause survives termination, the agreement could be terminated (even deliberately in the circumstance where the counterparty itself breaches) and the counterparty could claim its indemnification obligation ended when the agreement was terminated. Since you do not have a crystal ball and do not know when a third-party claim will arise, make sure the indemnification clause survives termination of the agreement. The language simply says:

> The indemnification obligations contained in this Section shall survive the termination or expiration of this Agreement.

Such language can be inserted at the end of an indemnification clause or in a separate survival clause that sets forth all terms that survive contract termination.

Traps for the Unwary When the Indemnity Process Is Not Followed

Parties often predetermine a process to follow should an indemnity obligation arise in the future. It is a good idea to outline rules of the road should a claim trigger indemnification. For example, parties are usually better off answering questions of who will retain counsel and whether to include any restrictions on settling claims on the indemnified party's behalf ahead of time. Below is an example of standard language describing indemnification procedures:

> *Upon the assertion of any third-party claim that may give rise to a claim of indemnity, the Party seeking indemnity (the "Indemnified Party") shall give the other Party (the "Indemnifying Party") prompt written notice of such a claim, and shall give the Indemnifying Party reasonable opportunity to settle or defend the claim with counsel of its own choosing. The Indemnified Party shall cooperate, at the expense of the Indemnifying Party, with the Indemnifying Party and its counsel in the defense of any claim and the Indemnified Party shall at all times have the right to participate fully, at its own expense, with counsel of its own choosing, in the defense of any such claim. Parties shall render to each other such assistance as may be reasonably requested to defend against any such claim. The Indemnifying Party shall not settle any such claim that results in an admission of liability or wrongdoing on the part of the Indemnified Party without the prior written permission of the Indemnified Party.*

As is typical, procedural clauses for indemnities address the topics of providing notice when a third-party claim is asserted, selection of counsel, right for the indemnified party to participate in the defense, cooperation between the parties, and restrictions for settling any claim. These cover the basic "what happens now" questions both parties will be asking should indemnity rights be triggered.

Of particular importance is the last sentence set forth above. It essentially prevents the indemnifying party from agreeing to a settlement stating that its counterparty committed wrongdoing. In practice, the indemnified party can lose control over the defense of a third-party lawsuit and wants to protect itself against any admissions of liability made on its behalf. Surely, admitting wrongdoing may not be in the indemnified party's best interest. In other words, if you are the indemnified party, you are essentially saying: "If you are going to sell me down the river for a settlement by stipulating that I committed wrongdoing, you will first need my written consent (which I will likely not give)."

While the above indemnity procedure language sets forth a road map for indemnity obligations, you want to beware of language that seeks to take away indemnification rights if the road map is not perfectly followed. For example, the contract could provide a party's obligation to indemnify is dependent (or conditioned) on the other party giving prompt written notice of a third-party claim. A party can then attempt to excuse its indemnifying obligations if the other party provides late or defective notice. Such language can look like this:

> A Party's agreement to indemnify, defend, and hold harmless under this section is conditioned upon the Indemnified Party providing written notice to the Indemnifying Party of any claim, as soon as reasonably possible, and in any event no later than within fourteen (14) days after the Indemnified Party has knowledge of the applicable claim.

While describing indemnification procedures is good practice, beware of conditional language that could result in a party forfeiting its indemnification rights altogether. The counterparty may justify this language by arguing, should a third-party claim arise and it is obligated to indemnify, it needs to know about the claim right away so it can properly defend the matter. The counterparty will take the position that an indemnifying party needs to promptly react and limit its liability should a third-party claim arise. But, the risk of unintentionally losing indemnification rights can be too great, especially if you are the one with a higher chance of seeking indemnification.

In practice, this conditional language can give a counterparty room to dodge responsibility on a technicality. This is not what you want if you are expecting to be indemnified. For this reason, if you see this conditional language, consider crossing it out or adding language clarifying that, while the procedures may be in place, an indemnity obligation is not forfeited so easily. The language looks like this:

> *Notwithstanding the foregoing, the conditions expressed in this section shall only apply if the Party demonstrates it was prejudiced by the delay.*

OR

> *Notwithstanding the foregoing, failure to notify promptly does not relieve a Party of any liability that Party may have, except to the extent that such failure materially prejudices such Party's legal rights.*

Confidentiality Provisions

If you are sharing confidential information with your counterparty, you will want to agree on clauses that provide you protection against the unauthorized use and disclosure of such information. Basically, parties typically set forth confidentiality provisions to ensure any proprietary information shared between parties will be kept secret.

Most times, parties have already entered into an agreement commonly referred to as a Non-Disclosure Agreement or an "NDA," which governs the exchange of confidential information between parties. This often happens even before parties agree to work together. There is a chapter later in this book dedicated to walking through the provisions of a typical NDA. Practically speaking, the provisions of an NDA are not dissimilar to confidentiality provisions found in the business contract. Indeed, if parties have already executed an NDA, they can avoid negotiating new confidentiality provisions in the business contract and simply incorporate the NDA into the contract by reference. This standard practice involves adding the following language to a confidentiality clause:

> The Parties acknowledge that they entered into a Non-Disclosure Agreement dated as of [insert date] (the "NDA"). The Parties hereby agree that the NDA entered into by and between the Parties is incorporated herein by reference and shall continue in full force and effect and shall apply to all Confidential Information (as defined in the NDA) disclosed by the Parties for purposes of this Agreement.

Should parties decide to go this route, one practice point is to refer to the NDA in the "entire agreement clause," discussed later in the book addressing General or Miscellaneous Terms. It is common for an entire agreement clause to include all documents between parties related to the business arrangement. Thus, since the NDA is such a document, it should be included.

Expressly noting the NDA as a document that pertains to the parties' deal is good practice and reiterates the parties intended for the NDA to govern confidentiality. Even better practice is to go one step further and attach the NDA as an exhibit to the agreement so that all documents relevant to the parties' business contract are together in one place.

But, what if you have not executed an NDA, and the parties are at square one with respect to confidentiality protections? No big deal. A confidentiality provision takes a similar format in most business contracts and can be easily understood. In its basic form, a confidentiality provision essentially addresses three questions. First, what information is considered confidential and needs to be protected? Second, what materials are not really secretive and therefore should not be included as protected confidential information? Third, what are the restrictions placed on receiving parties (or a single party, if there is only one party receiving information), with respect to the exchange of confidential information? The confidentiality clause typically answers those questions in that order. Let's break it down.

What Information Is Considered Confidential?

At the outset, you should consider what information, if any, you may disclose to the other party that you don't want shared with others. Nearly all confidentiality provisions start out with a clause stating parties will not disclose confidential information and will expressly define what that entails. For example, the provision will look something like this:

> *Either Party may disclose Confidential Information to the other Party during the Term of this Agreement. "Confidential Information" means all information disclosed by one Party ("Disclosing Party") to the other Party ("Receiving Party") that is labeled "Confidential" or the like, or that reasonably should be understood to be confidential given the nature of the information and the circumstances of the disclosure. The following information will be considered Confidential Information whether or not marked or identified as such [insert information that could be disclosed, such as any trade secrets and/or other proprietary, non-public information including any designs, prices, finances, technologies, marketing plans, product plans, pricing*

data, product designs, technology, software, sales information, customer lists, etc.].

In the above example, parties are laying out the types of information they expect could be exchanged and should be considered confidential information. If you are the disclosing party, you will tend to err on the side of wanting all information you disclose to be protected. For this reason, disclosing parties often throw in the kitchen sink of every possible category, drafting the broadest possible definition of confidential information they can think of. A disclosing party does not want to accidentally leave out any information that it may disclose and wants kept secret. Moreover, disclosing parties often also include language stating "oral" communications should be considered confidential information. This way, they are protected should sensitive information be communicated orally.

On the flip side, the receiving party may seek to limit the definition of confidential information. Think of it this way: If you are the receiving party, you may not want to agree everything you receive is suddenly confidential material and cannot be used for certain purposes or disclosed to others. To that end, the receiving party may cross out categories listed in the definition of confidential information that it finds vague or not relevant under the circumstances. Sometimes a receiving party will take a more extreme position and insist all information a disclosing party considers confidential in nature must be specifically labeled as such. In other words, the receiving party will demand only information designated confidential be treated as such.

Sure, it would be nice if the disclosing party labels every piece of information with a stamped "Confidential", but practically speaking, this may not be logistically feasible. In most cases, you can expect the disclosing party to push back on such a burdensome, and potentially unworkable, requirement. Unless, of course, there is a manageable volume of information being exchanged and circumstances allow for explicit marking of the information disclosed.

One last point to consider when reviewing this section of a confidentiality clause is whether the parties want to include the terms of the agreement themselves as confidential information. There are various reasons why parties may agree to maintain confidentiality of the agreement itself. For example, a seller may desire its prices are not disclosed, or a buyer may not want its competitors to know its supplier. Whichever the parties choose, if they end up agreeing to such language, actually abide by the restriction and remind employees to keep contract terms under wraps.

What Materials Are Not Really Secretive?

Despite what the disclosing party may think, not everything disclosed to the other party will be so secretive that it needs to be handled with care and entitled to restrictive disclosure and use provisions. Given this reality, in nearly all confidentiality clauses, parties set forth categories of information that do *not* need to be treated as confidential. In other words, certain information disclosed is excluded from the definition of confidential information for the simple reason it is not secret.

These categories of excluded information are found in nearly all confidentiality clauses. If it is not there, and you are the receiving party, add them. The categories tend to be routine, straightforward, and encompass the following topics. Confidential information does *not* include:

Publicly Available Information. Information that was publicly known before or after it was disclosed, if it was through no fault of the receiving party, is not considered confidential information. In other words, if information was or becomes generally known, and not because the receiving party disclosed the information, of course, it is not included as confidential information.

Information Already Known to Receiving Party. Information already known to and in the possession of the receiving party prior to receipt from the disclosing party is not considered confidential information. You may also see language that requires the receiving party to show, through its books and records, information was already known prior to disclosure. This way, the party cannot fabricate it had the information prior to disclosure, but rather is required to show actual evidence of its independent prior possession.

Third-Party Source. If the information was obtained from a third party, and that third party was free of any obligation of confidentiality (*i.e.*, that third party is not breaching an NDA or other confidentiality restrictions), information is not to be considered confidential information. The recipient has to rightfully receive the information from a third party.

Independently Developed by Receiving Party. If the information was independently developed by the receiving party without use of the confidential information, it would not be considered confidential information. You may also see language that requires the receiving party to show, through its books and records, information was independently developed by the receiving party. The disclosing party may seek to review actual evidence to verify such was the case.

Written Permission by Disclosing Party. Information specifically approved in writing by the disclosing party for the receiving party to release would not be considered confidential information. In effect, the disclosing party gave the receiving party permission, in writing, to disclose the information.

Putting this together, the exclusion language looks like this:

Confidential Information shall <u>*not*</u> *include any information that:*

i.   *was publicly known and made generally available in the public domain prior to the time of disclosure by the Disclosing Party;*

ii.   *becomes publicly known and made generally available after disclosure by the Disclosing Party to the Receiving Party through no action or inaction of the Receiving Party;*

iii.   *is already in the possession of the Receiving Party at the time of disclosure by the Disclosing Party;*

iv.   *becomes available to the Receiving Party on a non-confidential basis from a source not bound by confidentiality restrictions that cover the relevant information;*

v.   *is independently developed by the Receiving Party without use of or reference to the Disclosing Party's Confidential Information; or*

vi.   *Disclosing Party gave written permission to Receiving Party to disclose.*

What Are the Restrictions When Receiving Confidential Information?

In this part of a confidentiality clause, parties will plainly state the receiving party cannot disclose confidential information to third parties, unless agreed otherwise. This is where parties express that they want the confidential information to remain in strict confidence. "Don't give away my secrets." Parties can also specify that confidential information can be shared with employees or other parties to whom disclosure is necessary to perform obligations under the contract. In essence, the disclosing party is saying: "It's fine if you disclose to your employees or agents who need to know the confidential information to perform services hereunder, but please make sure they abide by the confidentiality restrictions." As a further matter, the disclosing party may want to make crystal clear that the information provided is its own, and they are not giving away any rights in the information to the other party. Also, the disclosing party is likely to restrict use of any of its confidential information for any purposes other than for effectuating services agreed to under the contract.

This part of a confidentiality clause typically looks like this:

All Confidential Information shall remain the sole property of Disclosing Party and Receiving Party shall have no rights to or in the Confidential Information. Receiving Party shall hold the Confidential Information in strict confidence and shall not use any Confidential Information of the Disclosing Party except as a necessary part of performing its obligations under this Agreement. Receiving Party shall not make any disclosure of the Confidential Information to any third party without the express written consent of Disclosing Party, except to employees, consultants or agents to whom disclosure is necessary to the performance of the Parties' obligations under this Agreement and who shall be bound by the terms hereof.

Lastly, parties often lay out a standard of care they expect the receiving party to adhere to when handling confidential information. Typically, parties agree the receiving party should protect confidential information to the same extent and by the same means that party protects its own confidential information. In other words, "treat my sensitive information as you would treat your own sensitive information." At a minimum, parties often set forth that confidential information should be handled with a "reasonable standard of care." Beware if you see some other, more stringent standard, such as requiring a receiving party to use "best efforts" to protect the confidentiality of the information disclosed. Unless a party is handing over a top-secret trade secret (*i.e.*, the *Coca Cola* recipe or *Google's* search algorithm), it is more common to stick with a "reasonable" standard of care. This part of a confidentiality clause can look like this:

> *Each Party shall take all actions as are reasonably necessary and appropriate to preserve and protect the Confidential Information of the other Party and such Party's respective rights therein, at all times exercising at least the same degree of care that it uses to protect its own Confidential Information of a similar nature, but in no event less than a reasonable degree of care.*

While the above sets forth common language found in confidentiality provisions, parties can agree to more extensive protections depending on the sensitivity of information exchanged between parties. Further analysis on mechanisms to protect confidential information disclosed by the parties is addressed later in this book in The NDA Explained chapter.

The Point:

- Confidentiality clauses are designed to keep confidential information exchanged between the parties secret.

- Most confidentiality clauses routinely contain language excluding certain categories of information not considered confidential, thereby not warranting special protections.

- Before agreeing to a confidentiality clause, determine whether you are more likely the party to disclose sensitive information or to receive sensitive information. This can shape your views on negotiating language that protects you under the circumstances.

Data Security and Privacy

As we enter the era of Big Data, companies are rapidly collecting and analyzing personal information about consumer activity. One of the questions you want to ask when reviewing a business contract is whether any of the parties are accessing, collecting or transferring personally identifiable information. If so, does the agreement have adequate protections?

Companies are currently facing a murky legal environment with changing privacy laws and data security regulations. What you may not realize is that many of these relatively new regulations are focused on ensuring that parties who transfer data between themselves have instituted contractual protections with respect to the collection, storage, use and transfer of data. In other words, you can expect in the future that regulators (whether domestically or abroad) will come knocking with requests to review commercial contracts related to the handling of personally identifiable data. Thus, you want to be prepared.

Negotiating data security provisions can be critical in guarding business information, as well as protecting against substantial legal and reputational exposures, should information be disclosed without authorization. It feels like every day a new company is announcing that its systems were hacked. Indeed, many of the recent hackings have stemmed from a vendor or commercial contractor obtaining access to personally identifiable information stored on the servers of the business. In other words, the hacker obtained access to the company's systems through the missteps of the contractor. Given the importance and seriousness of data security clauses, it should come as no surprise that they can be more complex than other routine commercial clauses addressed throughout this book.

We can work to break down the basic parts in data security clauses; however, given that this is such a relatively new area of law, it is still evolving and there are no standardized, boilerplate terms yet to emerge. Generally speaking, there are essentially two types of information receiving the most attention in business contracts.

> **Personally Identifiable Information.** A broad definition of Personally Identifiable Information, or what is known as "PII", includes first names, last names, email addresses, mailing address, account numbers, or any information that may be used to track, locate or identify an individual (or which is otherwise protected by law).

> **Personal Financial Information** relates to credit card numbers, debit card numbers, bank account information, security codes, passwords, and other consumer financial information.

Just to be clear, the above categories are not intended to be exhaustive. If you are in a business that receives sensitive information, such as obtaining healthcare records, other financial records or social security numbers, you will probably want to negotiate heightened protections. But, for more routine business transactions, it is typical for data security provisions to be based on the sharing of PII or personal financial information.

Once you have determined the parties will be sharing either of these forms of consumer data, PII or personal financial information, you will need to understand who will have ownership rights to the data and what type of secure practices will be in place to protect against unauthorized disclosure. Below are general topics and example clauses you may consider implementing in a business contract.

Securing PII from Unauthorized Disclosure

When your counterparty has access to PII because of the business relationship, you will want to ensure it is keeping information secure. Language typically incorporated into a business contract is similar to the confidentiality provisions discussed earlier. A provision seeking to secure PII from unauthorized disclosure can look like this:

> *Receiving Party agrees that it shall use commercially reasonable efforts to keep and maintain all PII in strict confidence, using such degree of care as is appropriate to avoid unauthorized access, use or disclosure. Receiving Party shall use or disclose PII solely and exclusively for the purposes for which the PII, or access to it, is provided pursuant to the terms and conditions of this Agreement. Receiving Party shall not use, sell, rent, transfer, distribute, or otherwise disclose to a third party any PII, unless otherwise agreed to herein.*

In the above clause, PII will typically be a defined term, which will include a broad definition of the personal and confidential information that the parties are accessing or sharing. Moreover, if both parties are exchanging information, the clause above should be made mutual so the parties have reciprocal obligations to maintain the confidentiality of each other's sensitive information.

Complying with Privacy and Data Protection Laws

Another provision commonplace in circumstances where PII is shared relates to the receiving party's compliance with applicable privacy and data security laws. You may notice a general statement of compliance with laws given that the laws are still being enacted. Such language looks like this:

> *Receiving Party represents and warrants that its collection, access, use, storage, disposal and disclosure of PII does and will comply with all applicable federal and state privacy and data protection laws.*

AND/OR

> *Receiving Party shall comply with the terms and conditions set forth in this Agreement and with all applicable laws, rules and legal requirements in its collection, receipt, transmission, storage, disposal, use and disclosure of such PII and be responsible for the unauthorized collection, receipt, transmission, access, storage, disposal, use and disclosure of PII under its control or in its possession.*

In addition to the above language, parties are also protecting against the transfer of personal information outside of the United States, where privacy and data security laws are different. For example, European regulations are often stricter than laws of the United States when policing the transferring of personal data. To protect against the transfer of data to other countries, you may see language providing that, *"Party shall not transfer any PII outside the United States of America without prior written consent of the other Party."* Given the different regulatory regimes currently policing the collection and use of PII, contracting parties are seeking to limit exposures by mandating the information stay within the confines of the applicable country.

Moreover, with respect to credit card information, there are extra provisions that may be applicable. The major credit card companies, such as Visa, MasterCard and American Express, have set industry standards referred to as Payment Card Industry Data Security Standards ("PCI") regarding the collection of credit card information. Given this, businesses may require their commercial partners are PCI certified if they are handling credit card information. Such language looks like this:

> *Receiving Party shall comply with the Payment Card Industry Data Security Standards ("PCI"). Upon request by Disclosing Party, Receiving Party shall provide Disclosing Party a certification, together with any supporting documentation, evidencing PCI compliance.*

Who Owns the Data?

If parties are transferring data to each other, they will want to discuss data ownership. A business contract should clearly set out who owns the data to avoid confusion as to the parties' intentions and uses of the data. If the party disclosing the PII will own the data, including any data that arises from the business relationship, then the disclosing party may add the following language to the business contract:

> *As between the Parties, Disclosing Party will own all right, title, and interest in and to all PII collected by Disclosing Party or Receiving Party in connection with the services provided under the Agreement.*

Without express language defining which parties own the data and how it can be used, a party can face legal and commercial consequences. You may uncover the opposing party selling personal data it collects from your company, and that could go against your business interests and expose you to liabilities. For example, if your counterparty sells PII collected pursuant to the business arrangement to third parties, you may be violating your company's privacy policy (*i.e.*, the public document describing how your business collects and uses PII). For this reason, in cases where PII is exchanged, a company may require the opposing party to review and agree to comply with its privacy policy. Also standard is for a party to include a link to the privacy policy that must be followed. Put simply, whenever parties are sharing or generating PII, in this day and age, it is prudent to set ground rules on who owns the data and specify how the data can be utilized.

Aggregated Data, Is This OK?

It has become increasingly common for a receiving party to add language allowing it to retain and use aggregated (*i.e.*, collected), anonymized data generated from the business relationship. The receiving party may seek to analyze the data and will promise it will be de-identified (no longer PII), explaining that aggregate data does not contain any information from which customers could be identified. The receiving party may insert language stating it alone owns all right, title and interest in and to aggregate data. Whether you choose to agree to allow the receiving party to collect and use aggregate data generated from your business depends on your particular circumstances.

Big Data is valuable. Suppliers and vendors may want to use aggregate data to enhance services or potentially sell data to others. As the party disclosing data, you will want to tread cautiously. At a minimum, ask a number of questions: What data will be aggregated? How will the data be used? Who will have access to the data? Will data be provided to your competitors? How is the data de-identified? These answers are important to obtaining a better understanding from the receiving party. Essentially, conduct due diligence before handing out your data.

Return or Destruction of Data

What happens when the contract ends or when the PII is no longer needed? Typically, parties include a provision that addresses a process to dispose of data. As with any shared confidential information, parties will want to consider adding language that makes clear the receiving party will, at the request of the disclosing party, return or delete the PII if practical. It is common to see the following language:

> *Receiving Party shall immediately, following a request by the Disclosing Party, at its discretion (i) return all PII to the Disclosing Party along with all copies or other records of the same; or (ii) destroy and/or delete all such PII and provide written confirmation of the same to the Disclosing Party.*

Audit of Security Procedures

While a disclosing party may be comfortable negotiating the above clauses in the contract, it also may desire to confirm the receiving party is abiding by its contractual promises. Because of the importance of data security, disclosing parties may seek to have audit rights to check and confirm the receiving party is truly complying with its security obligations. The risks and exposures may be too high to rely solely on contractual language alone. A general and broad audit provision would look like the below; however, a party can also draft a more detailed audit provision that sets out specific processes and procedures.

> *Disclosing Party reserves the right upon giving reasonable notice and within normal business hours to*

require such reasonable rights of access and audit as may be needed to assess other Party's compliance with its obligations set out in this Agreement in respect of PII.

Process if Security Breached

Finally, parties will want to formulate a plan if a doomsday scenario unfolds. Should a receiving party incur a security breach, the disclosing party will want to spring into action to mitigate the problem. If the breach was serious, the disclosing party is likely in crisis mode. The last thing a disclosing party wants in those circumstances is to be arguing with the other party about its rights to obtain information and access about what happened. Thus, a disclosing party can plan ahead and draft language, such as the below, which sets forth its rights to obtain immediate access from the receiving party to fully investigate the security breach.

In the event of any security breach relating to PII, Receiving Party shall notify Disclosing Party immediately. Immediately following Receiving Party's notification to the Disclosing Party of a security breach, the Parties shall coordinate with each other in good faith to investigate the security breach. Receiving Party agrees to fully cooperate with Disclosing Party, including, without limitation: (i) assisting with any investigation; (ii) providing Disclosing Party and its advisors with physical access to the operations affected; (iii) facilitating interviews with Receiving Party's employees and others involved in the matter; and (iv) making available all relevant records, logs, files, data reporting and other materials required to comply with applicable law, regulation, industry standards or as otherwise reasonably required by Disclosing Party.

Receiving Party shall at its own expense use commercially reasonable efforts to immediately contain and remedy any security breach and prevent any further security breach, including, but not limited to taking any and all action necessary to comply with applicable privacy rights, laws, regulations and standards.

Having a process in place to address data breaches is smart; however, making sure you can recover from the other party any losses suffered following a breach is smarter. When a data breach occurs, the costs can be staggering and amass quickly. There will be costs for notifying the affected persons and possibly providing credit monitoring services, as well as costs for recreating or reloading lost or stolen data, public relations costs for fixing reputational damages, legal costs to work with regulators and resolve potential lawsuits, forensic services to remediate the breach, and, perhaps the biggest financial consequence, lost business as consumers lose trust. The list of costs and losses from a data breach can go on and on.

In order to protect yourself, as discussed earlier in the book, you have to negotiate a limitation of liability clause that does not restrict your recovery of potential losses. You also want to agree on a fair indemnification provision to foot the bill for any third-party claims or government fines. Thus, the takeaway is that, should you be sharing PII, personal financial information, or other sensitive data, having commitments by the other party to keep data safe is important. But, if you don't bargain for sufficient liability coverage—scrutinizing both the limitation of liability and indemnification clauses—to provide you recovery in the event of a data breach, you can be leaving yourself exposed. BIG TIME. In other words, the above data security clauses are not worth much if you are on the hook to pay for a data breach.

The Point:

- Data security clauses are becoming increasingly popular in light of heightened awareness of risks surrounding collection, use and disclosure of personally identifiable information and other sensitive data.

- When entering into a new business relationship, make sure to consider whether the parties will be exchanging consumer or other types of personally identifiable data. If so, include data security and privacy clauses.

- Put yourself ahead of the curve. As data security regulations unfold, you will be appreciative that you negotiated data security protections and knew to bargain for liability coverage in case of a data breach.

Force Majeure Clause

Typically, there is one clause in a contract that prepares parties for the worst. For example, what happens if an earthquake damages your company's manufacturing facility and, as a result, you are unable to fulfill your duties under the agreement? Or, what if a terrorist attack impacts your ability to perform under the agreement? When negotiating a business contract, parties often prepare for the possibility that, while remote, they may be faced with unforeseen circumstances beyond their control that can prevent them from performing under the contract. To that point, it is commonplace to find a clause in the contract, often entitled, "force majeure," referred to colloquially as a superior force, an unexpected event, or act of God.

The purpose of a force majeure clause is to excuse a party from performance under the contract where there has been an unforeseeable disaster or unanticipated external event. In other words, if a party cannot perform under the agreement because of an unforeseen catastrophic event, such party can point to a force majeure clause to excuse its performance or defend against a claim it breached the contract. A force majeure clause is often considered a standard clause, providing the following:

> *Any delay in or failure by either Party in performance of this Agreement shall be excused if and to the extent such delay or failure is caused by occurrences beyond the reasonable control of the affected Party including, but not limited to, decrees or restraints of government, acts of God (e.g., hurricane, earthquake, tornado, flood), fire, explosion, terrorism or threats of terrorism or war (each being a "Force Majeure Event").*

In essence, a force majeure clause describes those uncontrollable events (such as war and threats of terrorism) and acts of God (extreme weather and unpredictable natural events) that are not the fault of any party and make it difficult or impossible to perform under the contract or carry out normal business. Parties often insert a force majeure clause into a contract to excuse performance under the contract and attempt to absolve itself from liability in the event it cannot perform the terms of a contract for reasons beyond its reasonable control.

With that said, in certain circumstances, parties may choose to adopt a more lenient standard that discharges a party of its contractual obligations if an event renders performance commercially impracticable (as opposed to impossible). That is, the parties can agree that performance is excused when it is not practical and can be done only at an excessive and unreasonable cost. The parties can also draft language providing for protection from a specific impediment that is defined in the clause. Whatever language ultimately selected, read the force majeure clause carefully to ensure it appropriately specifies the parties' understanding of when performance can be delayed or excused.

What to Watch Out for in a Force Majeure Clause

There are basically five things to keep in mind when reviewing a force majeure clause. First, read the examples provided as uncontrollable events and confirm you agree with the list. If you might rely on a force majeure clause, the more specific you are as to the events covered under the clause, the better the contract will protect you. It is in your interest to specify any circumstances you anticipate could prevent or impede your performance of the contract. This is because if that specific event occurs, you can point to language describing it and have a solid argument such was expressly set out in the force majeure clause.

On the flip side, watch out for your counterparty inserting examples that are not actually unforeseen events beyond its control. A supplier will tend to draft a broader force majeure clause, while a consumer may prefer to keep it narrowly focused. Be careful not to agree to a wide range of matters, such as internal matters, that under the circumstances may not be true force majeure events.

For example, you may prefer not to excuse performance of the other party due to computer failures when you are contracting with a company for the purpose of providing computer services. Or, if you are hiring a firm to provide you labor intensive services, you may be hesitant to consider a labor strike or a labor dispute as a force majeure event. Presumably that firm has control over its employees. In effect, read the list of excusable events carefully, and cross out those that are truly not beyond the other party's control or are issues that can be resolved.

Second, make sure the clause is mutual. Both parties should receive protection from uncontrollable events. If you come across a clause that only allows one party to claim a force majeure event, modify the language so it protects you as well.

Third, consider adding language that allows you to terminate the contract in the event of a force majeure event. Practically speaking, a clause may provide that a party's obligation to perform under the agreement is temporarily suspended during a force majeure event. Depending on your business needs, you may desire to exit the agreement altogether should the force majeure event continue for an extended period of time, as you may need another supplier. You want to avoid being in "limbo" indefinitely (whereby the contract is not being performed, but neither party is in breach). For this reason, parties negotiate that the agreement can be terminated if the force majeure event continues for a prescribed period of time. An example of a force majeure clause that allows a party to terminate is the following:

> *Neither Party shall be held responsible for any delay or failure in performance of any part of this Agreement to the extent such delay or failure is caused by fire, flood, explosion, war, embargo, government requirement, civil or military authority, act of God, or other similar causes beyond its control and without the fault or negligence of the delayed or non-performing Party. The affected Party will notify the other Party in writing within ten (10) days after the beginning of any such cause that would affect its performance. Notwithstanding, if a Party's performance is delayed for a period exceeding thirty (30) days from the date the other Party receives notice under this paragraph, the non-affected Party will have the right, without any*

liability to the other Party, to terminate this Agreement.

Fourth, most force majeure clauses require an affected party to promptly notify the other party if it becomes aware of a force majeure event. Thus, practically speaking, should an unforeseen event arise that prevents a party from satisfying its contractual obligations, it will want to give proper notice. How a party provides proper notice pursuant to the contract is discussed in the notice clause (addressed later in this book). If you fail to provide proper notice, you may not be able to successfully declare a force majeure event, and may be in breach of contract. Don't assume because everyone knows about the event that notice provisions can be disregarded.

Finally, watch out for a party attempting to inappropriately invoke a force majeure clause to weasel out of contractual obligations. A party may claim that a force majeure event arose when, in fact, the contract has become burdensome or unprofitable for that party. But a deal is a deal. Those are risks the party undertook when entering into a contract. In short, a force majeure clause should not be used as an exit strategy or as an improper excuse to not fully perform under the agreement.

The Point:

- The premise of a force majeure clause is to excuse performance of a contract, either permanently or for a period of time, due to unforeseen circumstances beyond a party's control, such as natural disasters and terrorism.

- When drafting and reviewing a force majeure clause, pay attention to the categories of events that are classified and defined as force majeure events. Make sure you are comfortable they

- accurately represent the scope of unforeseen events beyond a party's reasonable control.

- Be careful of a party relying on a generic force majeure clause for tactical reasons to avoid its responsibilities to perform under the contract.

Assignment Clause

An assignment clause is premised on whether you want to permit your counterparty to transfer rights and obligations under the agreement to another entity. In other words, are you comfortable having a third party takeover the obligations of the business relationship. In most cases, who you are contracting with matters, and you may not want to allow that party to transfer or "assign" its rights to an unknown third party. Practically speaking, what if your counterparty assigns your contract to a party you dislike (maybe a competitor) or one you don't trust to pay the bills? You may desire to approve in advance any new party you could be working with under the agreement.

For this reason, it is typical for a contract to provide that a party cannot allow another party to take over the responsibilities and obligations under the agreement without prior written consent from the counterparty. Such is commonly referred to as an "anti-assignment" clause since a party is disallowing the other party to assign the agreement to a third party without obtaining prior written consent. A standard anti-assignment clause looks like this:

Neither Party may assign this Agreement, in whole or in part, without the other Party's prior written consent, and any attempted assignment without such consent will be void.

If you decide *not* to add the above language in your agreement, generally speaking, your counterparty may be able to assign the agreement without your permission. As a rule of thumb, in the absence of an anti-assignment clause (such as the above) the law generally permits parties to assign the contract freely, without consent of the other party.

There are, of course, exceptions to this rule. For example, what if you had a contract with Picasso to paint you a picture. Clearly, you don't want Picasso to assign the agreement to someone else. In effect, contracts that are more "personal in nature" and would go against the parties' intentions to allow assignment, may not follow the general rule that assignments are freely allowed. Nonetheless, given most contracts are implicitly freely assignable, it is commonplace to include an "anti-assignment" clause to prevent being stuck in a relationship with someone else.

The Point:

- An assignment clause addresses whether the contract can be transferred to a third party and to what extent consent is needed from your counterparty to make such transfer.

- Many contracts have what is called an "anti-assignment" clause that requires a party to obtain the counterparty's consent before transferring a contract to a third party. Without such language, the rule of thumb is that such transfers or assignments are generally allowed.

Anti-Assignment Clauses and the Sale of a Party

As mentioned above, anti-assignment clauses are common in agreements. Many contracts have boilerplate language that the parties should seek each other's prior written consent before transferring the rights of the contract to another. But, what if there are circumstances where it would not be practical to obtain consent when transferring the rights of an agreement? A common circumstance might be if one of the parties is acquired by another company. When that occurs, the party selling itself does not want to be forced to seek consent from every party it is under contract. If the selling party needed consent from all of its counterparties, such could potentially cause problems during the sale and create a serious headache.

There are many issues that could arise if you need to ask for consent from counterparties when selling your business. What if a counterparty that was a large customer or a landlord refuses to provide consent? What if a counterparty took advantage of your need to obtain its consent and used it as leverage to extort concessions in return for its consent? Without the ability to assign business contracts over to the new acquirer, the sale of your company could be made more difficult and put you in a sticky situation. While you were hoping for a smooth transaction and counting your money on a lucrative deal, there could now be unwanted hiccups.

Given this, many contracts plan ahead and draft language to protect a party from the circumstance of a potential sale of such party, even if it is remote. One potential option is to add a few words at the end of the anti-assignment clause, stating consent *"cannot be unreasonably withheld or delayed"* by the other party. This would basically preserve a party's ability to contest its counterparty's actions should it withhold consent for bad faith or non-legitimate reasons. It allows the transferring party to come back with some leverage should the other party attempt to make it difficult for the party to transfer the agreement to another.

Practically speaking, this may not be enough. Your counterparty may be able to argue its withholding of consent is reasonable under the circumstances. If a party wants to withhold consent to extract concessions, it is unlikely to freely admit to doing so in bad faith. Rather, it may concoct a "legitimate" business reason for refusing consent and intentionally cause a dispute.

For more belt and suspenders, it is common for a party to add specific language in an assignment clause that expressly allows for the transfer of rights or assignment in the case of a purchase or acquisition of a party. The assignment provision commonly looks like this:

> *Notwithstanding the foregoing, either Party may assign this Agreement to an acquirer of such Party, whether such acquisition occurs directly or indirectly by merger, consolidation, by operation of law or other statutory process, by purchase of more than 50% of the voting power of the Party's outstanding equity securities or by purchase of all or substantially all the assets of such Party. Subject to the foregoing, this Agreement shall inure to the benefit of and be binding upon each Party's successors and permitted assigns.*

Or a shorter, less detailed, version:

> *Assignment is permitted to any successor by reason of merger, reorganization, sale of all or substantially all of the assets, change of control or operation of law.*

If you agree to these provisions, you are basically saying you will permit the contract to be assigned to the acquirer or resulting entity. You are essentially not requiring the other party to obtain your permission if another company takes over the business and steps into the shoes of your counterparty.

However, there is one extra step of precaution you can take in this circumstance should you permit assignment by merger or acquisition. If there is a chance that the counterparty will be acquired by a competitor, you can require consent prior to assignment in that limited circumstance. In other words, assert the following exclusion, *"provided that the assigning Party shall obtain the other Party's prior written consent in the event that the proposed assignee operates a business that is directly competitive with the business of such other Party."* Such language would at least provide you with a basis to avoid unintentionally ending up in a commercial arrangement with your direct competitor.

As a final point, if you already have anti-assignment clauses in your contracts, but they fail to include language allowing an assignment in case of a merger or acquisition, don't worry too much. There may be ways lawyers can structure a sale of a company to avoid triggering the need to obtain consent under an anti-assignment clause. For example, structuring a sale as a merger can, in many instances, reduce the need to obtain your counterparty's consent with respect to an anti-assignment clause. Certain complex merger structures (such as a reverse-triangular merger) may be employed to avoid triggering an anti-assignment clause and therefore the headaches of obtaining consents from business parties.

In sum, an anti-assignment clause that requires you to obtain consent before transferring a contract to a third party can, in theory, cause headaches when seeking to sell your business to another. Thus, adding extra language that allows assignments in a sale situation can be prudent. However, in practice, anti-assignment clauses can be a non-issue depending on how a sale is structured.

Forum Selection and Choice of Law Clause

In general, a forum selection clause addresses the laws to apply when interpreting a contract and designates the location and court to decide legal disputes. Specifically, the provision provides: (i) which state law governs the agreement, known as "choice of law;" (ii) where parties will be hauled into court should a dispute arise, known as "venue" and (iii) what court will have authority to hear the case, known as "jurisdiction." The venue chosen by parties could include a particular country, state or city where they agree in advance conflicts will be resolved.

A forum selection clause is often treated as boilerplate and taken for granted. Although, for practical reasons discussed below, it should be taken more seriously. A forum selection clause in a business contract typically looks like this:

> *This Agreement and all acts and transactions pursuant hereto and the rights and obligations of the Parties hereto shall be governed, construed and interpreted in accordance with the laws of the State of New York, without regard to its principles of conflicts of law. Both Parties agree that any legal action or proceeding arising out of or relating to this Agreement shall be brought and determined solely in any state or federal court of competent jurisdiction in New York County, New York. Each Party irrevocably submits to the exclusive jurisdiction of the aforesaid courts with regard to any legal action or proceeding arising out of or relating to this Agreement.*

You might say to yourself, why does it really matter which state you agree upon for venue (or location to resolve disputes) or governing law? What is the big deal? For example, business folks may take direction from legal that New York is the venue of choice and they should push for that state in negotiations; yet legal doesn't explain the reasons why this is important.

For starters, generally speaking, each state has its own body of contract law that is applied to interpret and enforce contract language. State laws vary and one state may be more favorable to a party than other states. A court in New York may be more likely to enforce particular provisions than, let's say, a court in California. Thus, a party may insist on a particular state law for the simple reason that it believes the laws of that state are more favorable to its contracting position. The same is true if a party chooses a particular international law to govern.

If your business is located in a certain state, you likely prefer any litigation dispute that arises between the parties takes place in that state. This is because you may feel more comfortable having a court within your area adjudicate disputes and hope for possible home court advantages. You may also be comfortable with the laws of the state you do business in and don't want to assume the risks and uncertainty of another, less understood, state's laws. If a party (or its legal counsel) does not have experience or knowledge of the state's laws, it makes sense for that party to be hesitant to agree to unfamiliar territory.

There are also practical reasons for choosing a particular state to be the venue or location of choice to handle disputes. Most legal departments employ attorneys that are barred in specific states and also work with outside attorneys who are barred in certain states. Due to professional practice rules, attorneys can only practice law in the state or states where they have a bar certification (*i.e.*, where they are authorized to practice law). Practically speaking, if you agree to a venue, such as Hawaii, and your attorney neither knows the laws nor can practice in Hawaii, you will be at a disadvantage should a dispute arise. The other side will have leverage over you if you are unfamiliar with contract laws in that state and have to go searching for an outside attorney in a foreign place.

Let's see how this plays out in practice. Take, for example, a New York business negotiating a contract with a third party located in Oregon. During negotiations, the New York business notices that the forum selection clause is marked up in the agreement. The counterparty crossed out the chosen laws and venue of New York and inserted Oregon instead. If the New York business accepts that change, it would be stuck with Oregon as the governing law and venue should a dispute arise and the parties head to court.

Now fast forward a few months, and an issue arises—let's say, the counterparty has not paid for the services agreed upon. The New York business goes to its trusted attorney, who likely practices in New York, and asks, what can we do? As part of the analysis, the New York attorney tells the party that because it agreed to an exclusive venue of Oregon, it will want to secure separate Oregon legal counsel. (Remember, attorneys are only authorized to practice law in the states for which they received legal certification). As a result, the New York business will incur increasing costs if the dispute escalates to litigation. The New York attorney may then offer to retain on the party's behalf, and work with, local Oregon counsel. But now the New York business is paying for two law firms.

The New York business will also come to learn that, should it pursue this dispute in court, the proceedings will take place in Oregon. Therefore, the party and any witnesses may have to fly across the country to litigate. This means even more money spent. The New York business quickly realizes the practical implications and negative consequences from picking a jurisdiction far from home. Now it may decide not to pursue legal action altogether, or accept a much lower settlement, as it recognizes the high costs of litigating in Oregon to resolve the dispute.

From the Oregon counterparty's vantage point, it recognizes the leverage it has under the circumstances and weighs that in evaluating the matter. Remember, the counterparty initially picked Oregon and, thus, has advantages. For example, the Oregon party likely has in-house attorneys already barred in Oregon who have familiarity with Oregon laws, knowledge of the court system, and who are more comfortable if a case is brought on its home turf. In short, the Oregon party has bargaining chips to benefit from the forum selection clause and can potentially resolve the matter without court intervention.

Alternatives if the Parties Cannot Agree on a Forum

Generally speaking, it is best for parties to agree in advance where to resolve conflicts before one actually arises. But what happens when parties cannot agree on a place to litigate disputes? There are various alternatives the parties can explore.

One option is to agree that a suit may be brought in either party's home jurisdiction. While this does not solve the problem of the New York business being hauled into Oregon should the counterparty bring a suit, it does provide the New York business with the option of commencing suit in New York should it decide to pursue legal action. However, this may create an incentive for the parties to race to their respective courts should a conflict arise, in an effort to be the one to first-file to get home-court advantage. Alternatively, parties could actually create a deterrent for litigation by agreeing that any action to resolve a dispute must be brought in the other party's home state. While not as common, such would make a party think twice before instituting litigation or racing to the court house in unfamiliar territory.

Another option is to eliminate the language that dictates an exclusive venue for the parties to litigate contractual disputes altogether. The benefit of not having a particular venue selected is that parties have optionality. The party who commences the suit (the plaintiff) is the party that initially chooses the venue or location for the court proceeding. Plaintiffs often forum shop for state or federal courts they find beneficial, sometimes selecting a venue that has favorable laws or judges to the party's legal position. If there is no agreed-upon venue to pursue disputes that arise under the agreement, a party can bring a suit where it desires, presuming the place has enough connections to the business arrangement. If the party chooses a remote location with no ties to the business relationship or the parties, the court can throw out a lawsuit in favor of a more appropriate venue.

The downside of leaving the venue open is that parties are exposed to the filing of lawsuits in unpredictable and inconvenient places. Parties also risk spending time and resources litigating which venue is more appropriate. In other words, if a party selects a venue that is not convenient for the other party, it is likely the inconvenienced party will complain to the court. In practical terms, this can result in expensive legal motions over where the parties should be litigating before the parties litigate the actual matters at hand. One of the parties will inevitably tactically file motion papers (*i.e.*, mounds of paperwork) to draw out the dispute. As a result, parties can face escalating legal costs for motion practice, as well as unnecessary delay. There is also the risk that without a selected forum, both parties could end up in messy and costly litigation in two states. Such could have been avoided had they agreed in advance to a single place to litigate disputes. Simply put, if you do not include a forum clause, expect that contractual disputes will be more expensive.

A third option is for parties to explore whether there is a neutral location and laws the parties both prefer. Sometimes both parties are incorporated in Delaware and may agree to use Delaware as the exclusive venue. Other times, parties may have offices across the country or world, and be able to mutually agree on a place. Finding common ground with respect to choosing a location for disputes is good practice and can be helpful in negotiations. However, if neither the parties nor the transaction has any relationship with the selected state, there is a risk a court could invalidate the choice-of-law provision. Although forum selection clauses are generally enforceable, a court could decline to enforce such a clause if the contract or parties do not have enough connection to the forum.

Get Real with Your Forum Selection Clause

One final point on forum selection clauses. Regardless of what the parties ultimately decide, keep in mind that a forum selection clause does not need to be a deal breaker. In practice, attorneys can spend an inordinate amount of time analyzing the forum selection clause, the chosen venue and the law for a particular contract. Some companies will even insist on applying laws of a state (or foreign country) that has no connection whatsoever to the place where parties are located or where the business will take place. While those companies may believe the laws proposed are more favorable, the opposing party will likely reject applying laws not connected to the party and the business relationship. Negotiating a venue or governing law unrelated to the parties or the services being provided could be viewed as impractical and unreasonable.

In short, over-lawyering and pursuing unreasonable forum selection clauses can lead to commercial delays when, in reality, the likelihood of a business relationship escalating to courtroom drama may be slim. In most cases, a forum selection clause does not need to be a road block to closing a business deal. As highlighted above, there are many compromises to explore when negotiating a forum selection clause. Moreover, as discussed next, parties can always decide to avoid the court system altogether and select alternative dispute resolution mechanisms to resolve disputes should they arise.

The Point:

- Forum selection clauses are highly useful in business contracts and can bring predictability to parties when disputes arise. However, if you have no clue what the laws are of the selected state, and do not have any attorneys to defend you in that state, it is probably not worth agreeing to the state, as it will likely be inconvenient and expensive should litigation arise.

- But, you can still attempt to compromise. If the counterparty will not agree to your home state, offer up both states. Consider whether you want to have no clause determining a particular venue. Explore other possible states that could work for both parties. Or, as discussed below, agree to alternative dispute resolution.

- Finally, don't forget that contract disputes are not typical. Most disputes settle and are resolved without litigation. Thus, a forum selection clause typically does not need to be a deal breaker, as hopefully parties will never face a dispute or will be able to resolve matters without litigation.

Alternative Dispute Resolution

Forget the public court systems. Parties may decide to handle disputes elsewhere. Instead of resolving conflicts in the courts, parties can agree on an alternative dispute resolution clause. For example, parties may choose to resolve disputes in mediation or arbitration instead of public courts. Mediation and arbitration may be common ground for both parties if they seek to keep disputes private and out of the public court system. "Let's deal with our disputes behind the scenes. No need to have our reputations tarnished." Many believe that if parties want to have any chance of salvaging their business relationship following a heated dispute, it is best to avoid publicized litigation that can often take months, or even years to resolve.

Arbitration

Arbitration can be an effective method to resolve contract disputes in a private setting. Once litigation is filed in the courts, parties can become emotionally charged and hostile toward one another. Arbitration, on the other hand, is generally held in private, allowing parties to avoid open courtroom drama and the nastiness that can come along with litigating disputes in public. Perhaps this is why arbitration clauses are frequently found in business contracts as an attractive alternative to litigation.

Parties can customize arbitration clauses in contracts to suit their needs. For example, parties typically agree in advance on which dispute resolution provider will handle arbitration. Most commonly used are the American Arbitration Association (AAA) and Judicial Arbitration and Mediation Services, Inc. (JAMS). Parties can stipulate whether they prefer a single, neutral arbitrator, or a panel of arbitrators, as well as the rules that would govern during arbitration.

A standard, simple and straightforward arbitration clause provided by JAMS for use in commercial contracts looks like the following:

> *Any dispute, claim or controversy arising out of or relating to this Agreement or the breach, termination, enforcement, interpretation or validity thereof, including the determination of the scope or applicability*

of this Agreement to arbitrate, shall be determined by arbitration in [insert the desired place of arbitration] before [one/three] arbitrator(s). The arbitration shall be administered by JAMS pursuant to its Comprehensive Arbitration Rules and Procedures and in accordance with the Expedited Procedures in those Rules. Judgment on the award may be entered in any court having jurisdiction. This clause shall not preclude the Parties from seeking provisional remedies in aid of arbitration from a court of appropriate jurisdiction.

Sometimes parties will craft language detailing specific qualifications for the selected arbitrator. For example, parties may require the arbitrator be a former or retired state or federal court judge, have a specified minimum number of years in practice, be experienced in a particular relevant industry, and/or have presided previously over a certain number of arbitration proceedings. Parties may agree to language similar to the following: "the arbitrator must be an attorney with a minimum of fifteen years of active practice in the entertainment industry." By doing so, parties are planning ahead to determine exactly what type of arbitrator they want resolving their disputes.

The Pros and Cons of Arbitration

Most people presume arbitration is cheaper, but this is not always the case. In an arbitration, parties will have to pay the arbitrator or a panel of arbitrators. This can be costly. Organizations that handle arbitrations, such as AAA and JAMS, charge parties fees to bring disputes and these can add up quickly. Moreover, as more experienced and sophisticated attorneys become arbitrators and charge higher fees, the costs of arbitration will likely rise in the future. That said, generally speaking, and depending on the circumstances, arbitration can result in a more cost-effective solution for parties than litigating in the courts. Court proceedings have their expensive components.

For example, it is well-known that arbitration often requires less documentary evidence and has limits on electronic discovery. When compared to litigating in courts, this can mean drastic cost savings. Nowadays with businesses creating voluminous document trails through emails and other electronic mediums of communication, it can be very expensive to preserve, collect, review and produce document discovery in litigation. Not to mention parties often disagree on what should be produced in discovery, causing motion practice in litigation that equates to higher legal costs. Sometimes the discovery process feels like it will last indefinitely, with parties filing mounds of paperwork and even deliberately playing games to inflict pain and escalate costs for the other side. Thus, agreeing to arbitration with informal evidentiary procedures and limitations on documentary evidence can be a means to save substantially on costs and resources.

Another benefit to arbitration is that parties will likely receive a faster decision in arbitration as opposed to the courts. If court dockets are crowded, which is often the case, parties can be delayed, waiting a very long time for a dispute to be heard and decided. It may not be in either party's interest to have a contract dispute delayed, especially if the parties are still working together. An arbitrator has more flexibility and can work with parties to schedule arbitration proceedings and resolve disputes both timely and efficiently.

Nonetheless, while an arbitrator's ruling can be more quickly delivered, it is important to keep in mind it can also be difficult to appeal. Put it this way: It can be nearly impossible to overturn an arbitration ruling should you dislike the outcome. Practically speaking, you can be stuck with the arbitrator's decision—good or bad. Oftentimes parties complain that arbitrators have a practice of "splitting the difference" when issuing an award. Also, arbitrators may award attorney's fees to the prevailing party in an arbitration proceeding, which can be costly for the other side and difficult to overturn. If you like the arbitrator's ruling, however, you will certainly be pleased to finally put the matter to rest.

Trying Mediation as a First Resort

Sometimes parties agree to commence mediation first to attempt to resolve a conflict privately with the help of a mediator. Providing mediation as an initial path can be cost-effective to resolving a conflict without resorting to expensive arbitration or litigation. A problem with insisting on mediation first is that mediation is only productive if both parties cooperate voluntarily. Thus, it can be a waste of time and resources if a party shows up to mediation without good faith intentions. But often, such is not the case. Once parties are at the table and talking through issues, an effective mediator can bridge the gaps between parties and resolve sticky situations. Mediation tends to be less adversarial than arbitration and litigation. The potential progress made when parties come together in a conference room and listen to one another's respective positions can be surprising.

In addition to mediation, there are a variety of other dispute resolution mechanisms parties can employ to avoid court room drama. Some companies include in their agreements an internal escalation process for resolving disputes. In effect, parties are required to attempt in good faith to address conflicts with appropriate senior decision makers before bringing a claim to arbitration or the courts. The agreement explicitly lays out a formal process to raise disputes to senior members with time periods built in to the resolution mechanism in hopes of a prompt resolution. This type of conflict resolution can feel like a waste of time if you are the non-breaching party. However, when it works, and the dispute is resolved promptly to both parties' satisfaction after senior decision makers weigh in on the conflict, it can be a home run. Parties can effectively avoid a costly fight, save on time and resources and potentially salvage the business relationship.

Ultimately, whether you prefer alternative dispute resolution or public court room fights depends on your calculation as to the odds of being the breaching party or suffering losses from the other party's breach. If you are more likely to be the non-breaching party, you may desire a public fight, or at least have the leverage to pursue litigation in the courts should the counterparty refuse to pay for your losses. However, if you are the party with a higher chance of breaching, you may prefer to quietly resolve disputes through alternative dispute resolution.

The Point:

- The court system is not always the right fit for parties to resolve disputes and choosing alternative dispute resolution can efficiently and privately resolve conflicts, thereby potentially preserving the business relationship.

- While selecting arbitration, mediation, or other forms of alternative dispute resolution as the adjudicator of choice can have its pros and cons, it is best to consider these factors in the context of whether you are the party more or less likely to suffer from a breach.

- Handling conflicts that may arise during a business arrangement through alternative dispute resolution may mean a quicker resolution with limited discovery and less lawyer time. A win-win for all involved.

CHAPTER 3

General or
Miscellaneous Terms

You have made it to what is typically the bottom section of a business contract. If you have read up until this point, you have shown a dedication to understanding business contracts. Well done! You are close to the finish line of being fully knowledgeable about the principal terms in business contracting.

This final part of a business contract typically involves a section entitled "Miscellaneous Terms" or "General Terms." In this section, loose ends are tied together and routine contract language is put in place. While this section may look like legalese to you, it is important to understand the premise behind these final clauses and be able to spot when they are not presented in a routine format. Often times these contract terms are crammed into a final paragraph. So, let's break down in simple form the common legal topics found in that last paragraph. You can bet that these remaining topics will be in nearly every business contract.

Amendment Clause

When executing a business contract, there should be a provision that addresses how parties can modify or amend the agreement in the future. Parties recognize that circumstances may change and they may desire to modify their initial agreement. As such, a business contract should always contain language that sets out the rules of how parties can modify or amend the agreement. Most of the time, parties will agree that any modifications must be in writing and signed by each of the respective parties. This essentially limits them from modifying the agreement unless an amendment is (i) mutually agreed upon and (ii) reflected in a written document signed by both parties. Having these safeguards in place prevents any confusion later on as to whether an agreement was purposefully modified by the parties.

An amendment clause is typically boilerplate and looks like this:

This Agreement may not be amended or modified except in writing signed by the Parties to this Agreement (or their authorized representatives).

Sometimes it can be the case that, for practical business reasons, parties agree that email modifications without actual signatures (or with e-signatures) will be sufficient. If you decide to allow for email modifications, weigh the pros and cons of a more informal amendment process. The pros are that parties do not need a formal legal document with signatures each time they want to modify terms. This can allow parties to efficiently and effectively change a business arrangement. For a fast-moving business, the ability to be more nimble and flexible with commercial contracting may be desirable.

There are also cons of allowing such practice. For example, you will want to make sure the person agreeing to an amendment via email is actually authorized to do so. Furthermore, because email modification is more informal, it can lead to mistakes, difficulty tracking amendments, and potentially issues of enforcement in the courts.

While an amendment clause may seem simple and straightforward, it is a key provision in a business arrangement. Should the contract fail to include such language, add it to the agreement so the parties have clear rules on how the contract can be modified.

Also, if you come across a provision that says something differently, such as the other party can amend the agreement without your prior written consent, seek clarification from your counterparty. For example, beware if you come across this type of language: *"Party may modify any of the terms and conditions of this Agreement, at any time in its sole discretion."* Such language is not common and may not be fair or reasonable under the circumstances. Think of it this way: If your counterparty can simply modify the agreement without your consent, then what is the point of mutually agreeing to terms in the first place?

For example, if the parties have negotiated over a price, an amendment provision that allows the seller to modify the terms without consent of the buyer can undercut those negotiations. The seller can hike up the price after the agreement is negotiated and signed, perhaps in the new year, when prices are adjusted for the seller's business. Given this, unless there is real justification for allowing amendments without mutual agreement in writing by both parties, you will want to avoid such a one-sided term.

The Point:

- Business contracts must contain language that provides how the parties can modify the contract should circumstances change in the future.

- Best practice is to have routine language that the agreement may be modified only by a writing signed by both parties.

Independent Contractor Clause

Business contracts, for the most part, state that the parties are "independent contractors." There are typically three reasons for inclusion of such language. The first is to set forth the independent nature of the parties' relationship and indicate there is no employment relationship between them. This effectively means one of the parties is not paying employment taxes (such as payroll taxes) or providing employment benefits on behalf of the other.

The independent contractor provision protects a party should the Internal Revenue Service (IRS) come knocking on its door to question its independent status with the counterparty. The independent status language can serve to establish to the IRS that the parties are not in an employee/employer relationship and intend to be independent from one another. This language clarifies the relationship of the parties and hopefully protects against any potential taxes and penalties.

The second reason for inclusion of such language is that the independent contractor clause sets boundaries that the other party is "independent" from you. It makes clear that the other party cannot act on your behalf and has no authority other than what is set forth in the agreement. In other words, you are telling the counterparty: "You cannot run around town acting as my agent. You cannot bind me to other obligations or incur liabilities on my behalf."

The third and final reason for this language is to avoid creating any special relationship between parties. By plainly stating that the parties are independent from one another, you are attempting to avoid any unwanted legal relationships. You are disclaiming that the parties have any special obligations to each other, such as owing fiduciary duties to one another, and that they can act independently as separate businesses.

Thus, putting this all together, a contract contains an independent contractor clause in order to (1) make clear that the parties are not in an employment relationship, (2) limit a party's authority to act on the other party's behalf and (3) disclaim any relationship status as anything but independent. The contract language is routine, boilerplate language that looks like this:

The Parties are independent contractors. Nothing in this Agreement or in the activities contemplated hereunder shall be deemed to create an agency, partnership, employment or joint venture relationship between the Parties.

If you are concerned that the parties can be mistaken as an employee/employer relationship or that your counterparty will exceed its authorization, you can add additional language to further clarify intentions. This language would include the following:

Nothing contained herein shall be deemed to create a relationship of employee or employer between the Parties. Neither Party has authorization to enter into any contracts, assume any obligations or make any warranties or representations on behalf of the other Party.

It is also important to note that you want to be careful not to use the word "employment" or refer to each other as "employees" anywhere in the agreement or elsewhere, as such language would contradict your independent status. Keep in mind, the label placed by parties on their relationship does not guarantee them independent contractor status. Practically speaking, if your relationship walks like an employment relationship and talks like an employment relationship, simply adding the independent contractor language may not protect you from a court or a government agency concluding differently. Thus, if the expectations are for the parties to be independent contractors, you can include the language above, but also make sure your actions are consistent with an independent relationship.

The Point:

- Independent contractor language provides that parties are independent from one another and signals they do not intend for an employee/employer relationship.

- Parties will be protected against being labeled as an employment relationship if they define their relationship as an independent contractor and the facts of their relationship support that conclusion.

- An independent contractor clause can also make clear that the other party does not have authority to act as your agent, enter into any other contractual obligations, or to incur any liability on your behalf.

Notice Clause

The notice clause addresses how one party is to notify the other pursuant to the agreement. A notice provision may seem insignificant at first glance, but it can be key to enforcing certain provisions. For example, what if you desire to terminate the agreement and need to tell the other party before an auto-renewal clause applies? What if an unforeseen force majeure event occurs and you are required to promptly notify the other side? Perhaps, you are seeking to notify your counterparty of a third-party claim to recoup indemnity costs. Or, the other party is in default, such as it has not paid in time, and you want to alert the other party about its noncompliance.

Given this, how do you provide such notice to the counterparty? It is simple. Find the notice provision in the contract and follow it.

A notice clause sets forth the logistics of providing notice to the other party, including the form notice must take, its method of delivery (email, fax, certified mail, *etc.*), when notice will be effective, and who must receive the notice. If you come across anything in a business contract that requires the parties to notify each other, turn to the notice clause and abide by its instructions. Without a notice clause in a contract, a tedious dispute can arise about whether notice was given properly to the other party.

A simple notice clause may look like this:

All notices, requests, directions or other communications hereunder shall be in writing and deemed to have been sufficiently given when delivered in person, by email, by a recognized national overnight courier service or by certified mail to the address of the respective Party below:

[Insert contact information of each of the parties or refer to the signature blocks of each of the parties set forth below]

If you want to be more specific, you can add timelines for each form of notice the parties agree upon. That way, it is crystal clear to all parties the exact date notice is deemed received and is thereby effective. Such language could look like this:

Any notices, requests, claims, demands or other communications required or permitted under, or otherwise made in connection with this Agreement, shall be in writing and shall be deemed to have been duly given (a) when delivered in person, (b) upon confirmation of receipt when transmitted by facsimile transmission or by electronic mail (but, in the case of electronic mail, only if followed by transmittal by national overnight courier for delivery on the next business day), (c) upon receipt after dispatch by registered or certified mail, postage prepaid or (d) on the next business day if transmitted by national overnight courier (with confirmation of delivery), in each case, addressed as hereinafter indicated.

There are just a few caveats to point out when reviewing a notice provision. The first is that you will want to confirm that the person receiving notice under the agreement is responsible and is the appropriate person to receive such communications. You can consider choosing the main business contact or legal counsel. Keep in mind that if you select your outside legal counsel as your contact, you may be charged if a notice is sent to your counsel. Outside counsel can charge fees for receiving and reviewing notices. By the time the outside counsel reviews the notice, sends you the notice and schedules a follow up call, you can accumulate legal costs, unless, of course, you have an arrangement with your counsel to not bill in those circumstances.

Second, it is commonplace to allow a party to modify the contact information because the company may move locations or the person authorized to receive notice may leave the company. To avoid falling under the formal amendment process of needing consent, a notice provision may include language to easily permit modifications. Typical language looks like this: *"These representatives and addresses may be changed by written notice given to the other Party."*

Third, consider whether you desire to permit notice to be provided by email, as opposed to more traditional methods, such as a physical mailing. On the one hand, to the extent the parties commonly deal with one another through email communications, the parties may find it easier to allow for notice to also be given through email. Some companies prefer to provide notice via email. On the other hand, notice is often required for terminating the agreement, to claim a breach of the agreement, or when a party is seeking to exercise its indemnification rights. Given the severity of these circumstances, you may prefer notice be formally provided, such as through a written letter sent by certified or overnight mail. Indeed, given overflowing email boxes, spam filters, and the possibility that an email can be easily deleted or missed, you may prefer more traditional methods of notice to ensure proper proof of delivery and receipt.

Regardless of how parties choose to provide notice, it is important to follow the terms of the notice provision when the agreement calls for you to notify the other party. Failure to abide with such a notice provision could impact your ability to enforce your rights or seek a remedy under the contract.

The Point:

- A notice clause informs parties how to give notice to one another in connection with the agreement.

- Should an issue arise and the agreement requires you to notify the other party, simply follow the notice clause.

Entire Agreement Clause

Parties often conclude business contracts with language providing that the contract constitutes the "entire agreement" between the parties. The reason for this language is simple: It is to prevent a party from claiming later on that it relied on other documents or oral communications apart from the final signed contract. Often referred to in legal terms as an integration (or merger) clause, the language provides that the parties intend for the agreement to be the final statement of their understanding, excluding any prior verbal or written agreements on the subject. This routine language found in most contracts says the following:

> This Agreement, along with any exhibits and schedules appended hereto, constitutes the entire agreement of the Parties regarding the subject matter of this Agreement and supersedes all previous and contemporaneous communications, representations or agreements regarding the subject matter of this Agreement, whether written or oral.

In effect, parties are saying: "This contract sets forth the complete and final terms agreed upon between the parties and any previous discussions or representations are superseded." The clause also essentially sends the message that a party should not rely on any earlier assurances or promises (whether written or oral) not integrated within the executed contract. In other words, "forget about what might have been said or promised earlier on or during negotiations. What matters is the final terms written in the contract."

In light of this clause, both parties will want to ensure all terms they agreed upon are set forth in the executed contract. Also, be sure the integration clause includes every document that is meant to be part of the agreement, including exhibits. Actually attach any and all exhibits and schedules to the agreement itself so they are all in one place.

In practice, a court will apply this integration clause to interpret the parties' intentions to confine their understanding to the contract itself. Generally speaking, a court can point to an entire agreement clause to preclude either party from introducing evidence of additional or inconsistent terms outside the four corners of the agreement. The purpose of an entire agreement clause is to preclude a party from digging out a long forgotten email to claim the other party promised something differently during negotiations. The court would rather stick to the agreement itself and not remarks made elsewhere. A court, however, could find an exception to this general rule when the contract is ambiguous, a party commits fraud, or if it made false or misleading statements during negotiations.

Nonetheless, it is important to realize you should not generally be relying upon conversations, emails or other correspondence to establish the terms of a deal. Any and all important terms should be set forth in the agreement. For best practices, if you have particular issues you want addressed in the contract, make sure to include it all in the final written agreement.

The Point:

- Nearly every business contract contains a clause that the agreement constitutes the "entire agreement".

- This prevents a party from relying on earlier promises not written into the agreement. It can result in a court focusing on the four corners of the contract when deciding a dispute.

- If a promise or representation is made during negotiations (whether in emails or during conversations), don't just take the other party's word. Verify it is memorialized in the agreement itself.

- Make sure to confirm all documents that are part of the agreement, including any agreed upon exhibits or schedules, are referred to in the entire agreement clause and are attached to the final documentation.

CHAPTER 4

Boilerplate Clauses

Boilerplate clauses are those same old terms universally found in almost every business contract. These are the clauses that, in practice, can be skimmed quickly without much time spent mulling over the language. They are so standard that you should not expect much variation from the language described below. You can hopefully check the box that these clauses were included and move on.

These clauses include (i) counterparts; (ii) severability; and (iii) general non-waiver. Given how standardized these clauses have become, we can address them briefly.

Counterparts

Ever wonder what language in a contract that talks about "counterparts" means? Probably not. But it is still good practice to understand this clause. Basically, in nearly all business contracts there is boilerplate language that looks like this:

This Agreement may be executed in any number of counterparts, each of which shall be an original, but all of which together shall constitute one instrument.

The above language essentially allows parties to sign and execute separate copies of the agreement. Back in the day (like, centuries ago), it may have been common for parties to sit in the same room and sign the same copy of an agreement. Today, business contracts are not typically signed in person with all parties present. Rather, they are sent back-and-forth by email and are not often signed in the same room, let alone the same piece of paper. To that end, the counterparts provision addresses the practical realities of the execution of the contract. It provides that the parties can each sign the agreement in different locations and such will count as if it was one original executed document.

In theory, absent a counterparts clause, a party could claim an agreement was not binding because it was not executed properly. A party could argue that the parties failed to obtain a single paper signed by all the parties. However, practically speaking, such is a weak argument. These days, your counterparty would have a hard time convincing a court that a business contract is not valid or legally binding because it was signed in multiple copies. In any event, because it is simple to include a counterparts provision, it is universally inserted in contracts to avoid any claims challenging the execution of the document.

Furthermore, given the use of computers and other technologies to make contracting more efficient, some parties are including additional language about executing agreements, such as by electronic means. For example, a party may input an extra line like this: *"Execution and delivery of this Agreement may be evidenced by electronic means."* Such language is meant to expressly set forth the parties' intention to allow for execution of the contract via an electronic form. The parties are effectively documenting their agreement to sign the contract electronically.

With that said, the law surrounding electronic signatures and execution of contracts through technological mediums is still evolving and not fully settled. Thus, if you are relying on electronic means to execute an agreement, you want to be careful. In addition to incorporating the language above, it is prudent to collect evidence that the electronic signature is the act of the person who purportedly signed the contract. Otherwise, you risk the other party claiming there was no formal acceptance and execution of the terms of the agreement.

The Point:

- A counterparts clause is boilerplate language inserted to allow parties to execute the agreement with separate copies in different locations.

- Do not waste much time reviewing a counterparts clause. Just accept it and move on.

- Should the parties decide to proceed with electronic signatures, include the parties' intentions explicitly in the agreement and collect evidence confirming electronic signatures are from the appropriate parties.

Severability

The severability clause regards how parties intend for the contract to be interpreted by the court in the event a dispute arises and a clause is found to be invalid. The clause basically permits a court to strike, or remove, an invalid clause and still keep the rest of the agreement intact. In effect, parties are telling the court: "If you strike down one of the clauses of this contract as invalid, perhaps because it goes against public policy or the law changed since the contract was entered, we ask that you preserve all of the other terms of this agreement." A severability clause typically looks like this:

If any provision or part of a provision in this Agreement is held to be illegal, invalid, or unenforceable by a court or other decision making authority of competent jurisdiction, then the remainder of the provision will be enforced so as to affect the intention of the Parties, and the validity and enforceability of all other provisions in this Agreement will not be affected or impaired.

Put simply, if parties agree to a provision that turns out to be invalid (for example, a non-compete clause can be found void against public policy), it makes sense for the parties to ask that the remainder of the agreement not also be invalidated. In practice, if you do not include a severability provision, you risk your counterparty seeking to void the entire agreement should even one provision be found invalid. Thus, in most circumstances, the above, rather boilerplate, severability clause is inserted to enforce the remaining terms of the agreement not found by a court to be void.

The Point:

- A severability clause permits a court to strike out language it finds invalid, while at the same time preserving the remaining terms of the agreement.

- A severability clause is boilerplate language usually agreed upon without much back and forth negotiation.

General Non-Waiver

Generally speaking, pursuant to basic legal principles, a party can inadvertently waive its rights under a contract by virtue of its conduct or inaction. A party may ignore that the counterparty breached a contract term, perhaps because it desires to maintain a friendly commercial relationship. However, such lack of action can be construed against the party. The counterparty could claim the other party "waived" (or relinquished) its rights and is prevented from seeking relief from the breach because it delayed or neglected to enforce its rights.

For example, a buyer could make a payment 45 days late. To the extent the seller permits this to continue without claiming breach, the buyer can argue the seller waived its rights to seek timely payments in the future. Thus, if by oversight or accident a party does not hold its counterparty accountable for a breach, the party risks relinquishing its rights to enforce the agreement and seek relief for that breach or potentially future breaches.

To prevent against an inadvertent waiver of any rights under an agreement, parties often include a routine, "non-waiver" provision in the agreement. This provision clarifies that any waivers of a term in the agreement must be set forth in writing by the party waiving such provision. A non-waiver provision may look like this:

> *The failure by either Party to enforce any provision of this Agreement will not constitute a waiver of future enforcement of that or any other provision. No waiver of any term, condition or obligation of this Agreement will be valid unless made in writing and signed by the Party waiving its rights.*

In this clause, the parties are stating that the failure of either party to insist, in any one or more instances, upon performance by the other of its obligations under the agreement, does not constitute a waiver or relinquishment of any such obligation in the future, and the agreement shall continue in full force and effect.

However, in reality, a general non-waiver provision is not necessarily bulletproof. Practically speaking, should a party breach a contract and the other party sits on its rights for an extended period of time, a court may look past the non-waiver clause and still find a waiver occurred. Stated differently, if a party elects to continue business and do nothing about a breach, the breaching party can argue successfully that the party abandoned its rights when it sat idle. A court often considers how a party behaved in the face of a breach. Sometimes actions speak louder than the words of a non-waiver clause.

The Point:

- A general non-waiver clause is routine, boilerplate language that seeks to prevent a party from using a counterparty's idleness as a means to claim the counterparty abandoned its rights under the agreement.

- Even with a non-waiver clause, a party's conduct in circumstances of a breach will likely still be considered, so don't remain silent or sit on your rights.

CHAPTER 5

Ten Common Pitfalls in a Business Contract

When entering into a business contract, many companies start out by providing their own one-sided template agreement. It can be frustrating when a company proposes a contract that unfairly favors only its interests. When this happens, a question burns through anyone reading the agreement: "You do realize there are two parties to this, right?" Sometimes, you can ask whether they have a different template, you know, one that includes mutually beneficially clauses and does not take hours to mark up. The response is typically "no".

Whether it is a good thing to commence discussions with a one-sided template is debatable. Surely, it requires parties to expend more time and resources to negotiate and can cause a partner to walk away, resulting in a lost opportunity. A more balanced agreement and mind set towards achieving a mutually fair business contract can result in substantial savings and more efficiency.

On the other hand, a one-sided template can provide the company who is pushing its template the most protection. It essentially forces the other party to work harder to negotiate rights for itself. The other party may sign away its rights or not spot potential pitfalls it is accepting in the agreement. Keep in mind, when reviewing a contract, it is just as important to understand what was *not* included in the draft as it is to spot the unfavorable language. Often times, what is left out, perhaps on purpose, can lead to an imbalanced agreement.

This chapter sets forth the red flags a party should be on the lookout for when reviewing another's template. The below highlights areas to be on your guard and gives pointers on how to avoid mistakes and potential problems that could surface later on.

1. Referring to Terms in Another Document

One practice you want to look out for when negotiating a business contract is when your counterparty references certain terms and conditions set forth in another document. The contract may include a link to other terms and conditions that requires you to copy and paste it into a web browser to review. You may also see a reference to other terms and conditions with language that they are "incorporated" within the agreement. It may look something like this:

> *This Agreement is subject to the general terms and conditions, located at http://www.com/sales/contract/ terms-and-conditions, which are hereby incorporated in this Agreement by this reference.*

Whatever form it takes, you have to be careful here. Think of it this way: If you are spending time negotiating an agreement, it may turn out to be fruitless if the other party is referencing a different document and claiming it also governs. Sometimes important terms can be hidden in separate referenced documents. So, what should you do? For starters, read the referenced terms and conditions. Make sure they do not conflict with what you have already agreed to with your counterparty.

Best practice is to insist that ALL terms and conditions the parties discuss be set forth in one document, for all to see, and to be executed together. This avoids any confusion about what the parties agreed to and keeps all of the terms in one complete document. It also avoids your counterparty amending or modifying the other terms and conditions as it pleases.

Ask your counterparty: "Hey, I saw you added a provision that references other terms and conditions that will govern our business relationship. Please provide me a copy so I can read them. Also, let's make it easier and append them to the agreement we are negotiating so we all know what we are signing. I would like to avoid any conflict or confusion, and I think working off one document makes sense."

If that does not work and the other party insists on referring to another document, at a minimum, there should be a provision that addresses how conflicts should be resolved. When referencing other documents, make sure the contract clearly indicates which document takes precedence in the event of an inconsistency. You can agree that, should there be a conflict between the currently negotiated agreement and other referenced terms, the *agreement* will govern and control. For example, such language looks like the following:

> *The terms of this Agreement shall control over any conflicting terms in any referenced agreement or document.*

OR

> *In the event of any inconsistency or conflict between this Agreement and an Exhibit, the terms and conditions*

of the Agreement will prevail and shall govern and control.

Should a party insert alternative language, such as that the terms and conditions of any exhibits or schedules (whether appended to the agreement or executed later on) will prevail, you want to be careful. Down the road the counterparty can slip in an unfavorable term in an exhibit or schedule that conflicts, or is inconsistent, with the agreement. When that happens, you can lose hard-bargained for rights.

In practice, you may be surprised to learn it is not unusual for a company to reference other terms in an agreement. Indeed, there are innocuous reasons why a company may reference other terms and conditions meant to be incorporated within the parties' document. You often see this practice with Internet companies who maintain their contractual terms on their websites.

Also, there are commercial reasons for referencing other terms in an agreement. It can make the agreement look much shorter and move business along without a ton of paperwork. Regardless of the reason, read those other terms carefully, include them in your discussions, and, if possible, append them to the final agreement.

The Point:

- Contracts may reference terms and conditions set forth in another document so beware of such practice.

- Read all terms and conditions that apply to the business relationship carefully and make sure they do not conflict with each other.

- If you can, append any and all referenced terms to the final executed document. Such would avoid potential confusion in the future, prevent your counterparty from modifying the terms without your consent, and keep all the agreed upon terms in one place.

2. Know the Party Who You Are Contracting with

Before you enter into an agreement with another party, make sure to check that you understand whom exactly you are contracting with prior to legally binding yourself to that person or entity. A business can often get caught up in "doing the deal" and reaping the benefits of a business opportunity. The business can be eager to sign an agreement without fully understanding whether the counterparty is reliable and safe to be a trusted business partner. Do not fall into this trap; rather, get to know your prospective business partner, conduct preliminary investigation work, ask for references and confirm such party is truly reliable. You may uncover information that causes you to have second thoughts about the other party.

In a worst-case scenario, should a dispute arise, you do not want to discover the entity you contracted with is a shell company or financially unstable and has no money to pay. In reality, a contract is only worth what the other party can pay to satisfy its obligations. You may have negotiated a favorable indemnification clause, but if the other party does not have the funds to cover the indemnity, you will be out of luck. Put it this way, if your counterparty does not have money to compensate you, your hard bargaining may turn out to be useless.

Below are simple practice points to follow when entering into a contract with a new business partner.

When contracting with a business, confirm the correct entities are listed. Parties to a contract should be properly and clearly identified upfront with their full legal names. Most commercial contracts commence with a paragraph that sets forth each of the parties' contact information, including names, addresses, and, for entities, sometimes state of incorporation. You should have an understanding of the exact entity that is the party to the agreement. You will want to confirm the stated party is the proper entity you intend to be legally bound.

Needless to say, always make sure a party's name is spelled correctly and includes the full corporate name (such as when the entity name contains an Inc., LLC, LLP or other suffix). This may seem obvious to you, but there may be times where you glance over the first paragraph and miss that the contracting entity is not whom you intended to be bound. Or, the contracting party includes other entities, like affiliates or subsidiaries, which you do not want to be part of the deal.

Additionally, be sure the party named in the agreement is in fact a proper legal entity. A simple search on the Secretary of State's webpage for the state where the business is incorporated can confirm the legal entity status. You don't want to discover down the road after a conflict arises that the entity named on your contract does not exist or is not sufficiently capitalized. If you are unsure about the other party's financial status, it is common to conduct a credit check to ascertain the credit-worthiness of the other party. Should the other party's credit check turn up red flags, you may reevaluate whether to partner with that party, or possibly ask for upfront payments or a deposit. Practically speaking, if the counterparty is not creditworthy or suffers a major financial set back during the agreement, your ability to collect under the agreement will be jeopardized.

Make sure the party signing the agreement is authorized to execute the agreement on behalf of the counterparty. It is best to avoid any questions about whether the person had sufficient authority to bind an entity on whose behalf the person signed. If you have never worked with the individual in the past, a Google or LinkedIn search of the person, a quick check on the company website, and/or a request of documents verifying the person's position within the company and authority to execute the agreement, is good practice. Most companies maintain records, such as a consent by the board of directors or other appropriate governing body, that sets out signing authorities within the company.

Moreover, having a more senior person in the company, such as the President or a person with a VP title, sign the agreement is typically safer. Officers of a company, generally speaking, often have signing authority. But, for significant or material contracts, do not always assume automatically the person has authority just on title alone. If that person does not have appropriate authority to sign on the entity's behalf, the entity can claim it is not responsible under the agreement. This puts you in an unpleasant situation.

Finally, if you want the other party to certify that it has authority to sign the contract, then do so. Whether in a separate clause (such as a representation and warranty, which we addressed earlier in the book) or prior to the signature line, it is common for a contract to affirmatively state that the party represents it is authorized to execute the contract on behalf of the entity. A typical representation and warranty looks like this:

Each Party represents and warrants to the other Party that it has full power and authority to execute and deliver this Agreement and to comply with the provisions of, and perform all its obligations and exercise all of its rights under, this Agreement.

Also, for added protection, you can insert the following sentence before the signature block:

The undersigned confirms that he/she has full power, authority and legal right to execute, deliver, and perform the provisions of this Agreement on behalf of Party and that this Agreement is legally binding upon Party in accordance with its terms.

Having these affirmative statements should give you more comfort, and perhaps legal ammunition, for relying in good faith on the person's authority to execute the agreement.

The Point:

- Know who you want to contract with and confirm such person or entity is the actual counterparty in the agreement. Failure to do your homework by conducting appropriate due diligence can be a costly mistake.

- Read the first paragraph of a business contract and make sure the counterparty's name is spelled correctly, contains the full and proper legal name, and is the appropriate person or entity.

- When contracting with a corporate entity, confirm the person who signs the agreement has authority to bind the entity and that the entity has enough funds to compensate you to fulfill the obligations under the agreement.

3.   Ensure the Executed Copy Contains the Final Agreed-upon Terms

During negotiations, parties may exchange various marked versions of the agreement and legal comparisons displaying the changes, known as blacklines. One practice point to keep in mind is to run your own blacklines throughout the process to ensure the changes noted properly reflect all changes made to prior versions. No matter how much you may trust the other side, always create your own blackline versions to feel comfortable that a change was not made that does not appear in the marked version.

Every once in a while there is a sneaky party who attempts to insert a modification without including it in the shared blackline. When you run your own blackline, you notice language was added or modified that was not in the version supplied to you. Follow-up conversations with that party are certainly not pleasant.

When parties have come to agreement on terms, there are a few simple, practical pointers to keep in mind before executing the contract. First, double check that all words capitalized and defined in the agreement are consistent throughout the agreement. Sometimes a party will forget to capitalize a defined word and this will inevitably create ambiguity.

For example, the parties may have capitalized and defined the term "Territory" to mean specific regions, such as North America and Canada. Should a clause accidentally use the lowercase word "territory," this can be interpreted differently with its ordinary, broader meaning being applied. A party may claim: "If we meant this clause to relate to those specific geographical locations, we would have capitalized the term territory, but we did not. The lower case speaks volumes and shows we meant the ordinary meaning. Let's pull out the dictionary."

In short, avoid a drafting disaster and conduct a final review of the agreement to verify that you have appropriately capitalized all defined terms. Moreover, if the agreement contains a definition section, check that all terms that are defined are moved into the definitions section. No need for silly mistakes that can cause discrepancies within business contracts.

If you are the primary drafter of the agreement, you can send a final version of the agreement to your counterparty once you have reviewed the contract for inconsistencies. Common practice is to deliver the final version for execution in a PDF form—and not in a Microsoft Word format or any other format that can be easily modified. The reason for this is to ensure the version you send with the final terms is not changed without your permission.

Also, when you receive a contract in PDF form following negotiations, it typically is a signal from the other party that it is not interested in further changes. This does not, however, mean you need to stop negotiating. Rather, it is a practice that some businesses employ to send a message that they would like you to sign the agreement as is. It can be perceived as a "take it or leave it" stance. If you are not comfortable executing the agreement at that stage, you can kindly remind the other party that the parties have not reached final agreement and you prefer to continue negotiating the document.

One mistake a party can make is to receive a template contract in PDF form and limit its review to only the provisions already within the agreement. Remember, that it is just as important to consider what clauses are omitted from the agreement. Do not assume the other party is providing a balanced and fair agreement. In most cases, they are not. Pay attention to what is missing in the document and needs to be added to protect your rights. Take a second pass through the agreement to avoid overlooking a key provision that was left out, perhaps deliberately.

Finally, if you are paranoid about the final version being altered by the other side without permission when you send the agreement for execution, there are other techniques you can employ. One practice is to initial each page of the document, then send a PDF to the other side for countersignature. By initialling each page, you can pretty much be certain the copy you receive back with the initials and countersignature was the same document you sent over for execution. Also, make sure when a final agreement is signed and exchanged between parties via email, both parties scan the entire document, not just the signature pages. That way, there is never a question as to what was actually signed and executed.

The Point:

- Review references to defined terms and make sure there are no inconsistencies within the agreement.

- Always make sure the executed version encompasses the parties' agreement and that no final edits were made to which you are unaware.

- Sending over a finalized PDF form of an agreement prior to execution is a common practice used to prevent unauthorized changes.

4. Shifting of Attorney's Fees: Good or Bad?

Sometimes business contracts include language that a party who breaches the agreement will pay the other side's lawyer's bills if it prevails in court. This is known as "fee shifting." Fee shifting is more common abroad, like in the United Kingdom. This is because the United Kingdom generally follows the "English Rule," which provides that the party who loses in court pays the other party's attorney's fees.

However, the United States generally follows the "American Rule," which provides that each party is responsible to pay its own attorney's fees, unless a statute or contract provides otherwise. Thus, while the general rule in the United States is for each party to pay its own attorney's fees, parties can choose to contract for a fee-shifting provision similar to the English Rule. The language would look like this:

> *In any legal action instituted by either of the Parties to enforce the terms of this Agreement, the prevailing Party shall be entitled to its attorney's fees and costs incurred in connection therewith.*

There are definitely different schools of thought on whether or not such provision is in your best interest. Should you keep it in the agreement or cross it out? Well, it depends on which side you end up on in a conflict. On the one hand, if your counterparty breaches the agreement, you may demand the counterparty make you whole with the damages you suffered. If the counterparty attempts to play hardball, you may like the idea that you have extra leverage to remind the counterparty that you will be seeking attorney's fees and expenses should you prevail in court. The fee-shifting provision essentially provides leverage to make the other side nervous, and perhaps more willing to settle.

Once a party knows it could be stuck paying for damages and high price tags of lawyer bills, such party may factor that in when deciding whether to bring litigation or resolve the matter. Truth be told, sometimes attorney's fees can be greater than the potential damages of the case. Moreover, in theory, a shifting of attorney's fees provision can discourage a party from bringing a frivolous lawsuit because the party filing the lawsuit risks paying the other party's legal bills. That notion alone could alter the parties' perspectives and positions.

That said, if you are the party that may have done something wrong, you will not like the idea of a fee-shifting provision. Now, you have to weigh the probability of losing the case *and* paying large sums of money for the other side's legal bills. Furthermore, circumstances can be murky and it may not be clear whether you breached the agreement in the first place. Maybe you did. Maybe you did not. In practice, often times it is not entirely clear under the law whether the other party will prevail in court. If it was, then parties would likely resolve the matter outside of court. Thus, what may be a close call on whether to fight or settle could become more challenging and worrisome due to a fee-shifting provision.

In short, a fee-shifting provision forces you to calculate these extra, and potentially substantial costs, as you decide whether to take the chance of defending the claim in court or risk having to pay for your opponent's legal bills on top of monetary damages. Suddenly, resolving the matter without court intervention may seem like the better choice. If you are a risk-adverse person, you may end up resolving a matter you would have otherwise fought because losing and paying your opponent's attorney's fees increases your exposure and potential money outlay.

The Point:

- The threat of having to pay your opponent's attorney's fees can provide powerful leverage to a party seeking to resolve a suit.

- A fee-shifting provision sounds great when you are the non-breaching party, but it is less appealing when the opposing party claims you did something wrong.

5. Don't Fall into the Trap of an Exclusivity Clause

Every once in a while a party may insert language attempting to restrict the counterparty from working with third parties, such as competitors, in the future. A party may seek to limit its counterparty from buying from other sources or engaging in similar business arrangements. The party may seek, for a period of time, for the counterparty to be prohibited from doing business with certain business partners.

From a supplier's perspective, it prefers the buyer show loyalty to its business. Moreover, the supplier would gain an advantage in the market if the buyer agreed to solely or exclusively purchase from the supplier and no one else. Given this, a supplier may include language in its commercial template known as an "exclusivity clause," which seeks to prohibit the buyer from working with others in the industry.

In addition to supplier agreements, these types of clauses are also utilized in service agreements. For example, exclusivity arrangements are common in the real estate market whereby a real estate agent seeks to restrict the homeowner or home buyer from working with others and requests an exclusive relationship. You will also notice these types of clauses in a recruiter engagement letter, which demands exclusivity as the recruiter expends resources searching for appropriate candidates.

An exclusivity clause will often set out a particular period of time of exclusivity and can also specify a subject matter and a territory restriction. However, there is no standard format an exclusivity provision resembles. Often times, an exclusivity provision will include the words "exclusive" or "sole" provider. An exclusivity clause can look like this:

> Party A hereby grants Party B, subject to the terms and conditions of this Agreement, the sole and exclusive right to provide the goods and services agreed to herein in the Territory (as defined below) during the term of this Agreement and any extensions thereof. Party A shall not enter into any agreements that would provide for services competing with Party B during the term of this Agreement without prior written approval of Party B.

You want to be careful not to overlook such a clause. An exclusivity clause can lead to problems and unpleasant surprises later on. If a party is not willing to provide exclusive rights to the supplier, perhaps because, as typically is the case, a party wants optionality to work with whomever it chooses, it should not agree to such a clause. While a party may initially prefer the supplier, over time the party may want to switch courses and work with competing companies. Moreover, an award of exclusivity may conflict with a contract a party has already executed or with the operations of the business.

At a minimum, a party faced with an exclusivity provision will want to consider three factors. First, the party should consider demanding additional compensation or discounts for exclusivity. If a party is forfeiting an opportunity to work with others, it should receive value for that concession. There is no need to provide exclusivity for free—it should be worth something.

Second, a party will want to read the exclusivity clause carefully and attempt to narrow the clause in scope, geography and duration. A party can negotiate potentially a shorter exclusivity period, a territory restriction, or fewer limitations in the clause. For example, a party can negotiate a set list of companies it will agree not to work with for a period of time, instead of agreeing to a blanket restriction of avoiding all competitors. Practically speaking, a party seeking exclusivity typically may only care about a handful of competing companies. Also, courts are more likely to enforce an exclusivity provision that names companies as it is more specific and clearly written. In addition, a party can negotiate a shorter time period of exclusivity, such as limiting restrictions to a few months instead of the full length of the contract term. Lastly, a party can seek to narrow the geographic limitation, choosing particular territories, and not agreeing to limitations throughout the entire world.

Third, a party will want to understand whether there are monetary payments owed if the exclusivity clause is violated. A clause could state that a party will face paying predetermined damages for breaching an exclusivity clause. If so, make sure to confirm that the potential damages are reasonable—*i.e.*, an amount enough to enforce the exclusivity provision, but not an egregious penalty.

Alternatively, if the buyer itself may compete with the supplier in the future, it may desire language expressly denouncing any exclusivity relationship. Such language would look like this:

The Parties acknowledge that the services being provided by supplier are on a non-exclusive basis. Nothing in this Agreement is intended nor shall be construed as creating any type of exclusive arrangement with supplier. For the avoidance of doubt, this Agreement shall not in any way restrict buyer from acquiring similar, equal or like goods and/or services from any other entities or third parties.

OR

This Agreement shall be non-exclusive and either Party may enter into any agreements with any third party for the same or similar services.

Practically speaking, such language is not as common and typically is only added in business contracts under certain circumstances. The first is where the seller raised the exclusivity issue, the buyer disagreed, and thereafter the buyer wants to make crystal clear that it is not agreeing to exclusivity so there is no dispute in the future. Another is where the buyer may engage in business endeavours that can be considered competitive to the seller. Accordingly, the buyer adds this language to avoid any attempts by the seller to restrict its relationships with third parties.

The Point:

- Exclusivity clauses may seem harmless at first glance, but they are not. Agreeing to an exclusivity clause may constrain a party from working with others and limit a party's freedom to contract with whomever it chooses.

- Before you agree to an exclusivity provision, confirm that the restrictions are acceptable and worth the amount you are compensated or value received.

- If you are opposed to providing any kind of exclusivity, you can add language denouncing exclusivity to make it clear in the agreement.

6. Do You Want to Be on the Hook for Lost Profits? It's Confusing

As discussed earlier in the book, in a limitation of liability clause, parties may agree to limit recovery they can seek following a breach of contract. Parties may negotiate that each will only be responsible for certain damages in case of a breach and not for others should things sour. Unfortunately, whether or not a party's lost profits are included within a limitation of liability clause, and therefore not recoverable, can be ambiguous and tricky.

Generally speaking, a party's lost profits after a breach can be considered either direct damages, which are usually recoverable, or consequential damages, which are often categorically waived in a limitation of liability clause and not recoverable. In practice, if parties don't think through this issue when negotiating the contract, it can result in ambiguity, leaving them to duke it out in court. As a result, parties can be stuck in an expensive dispute as they hire their respective lawyers and try to piece together whether they intended for lost profits to be recoverable.

For example, let's say you rented a booth at a rock concert to sell t-shirts specially designed for the show. You expect to make around $25,000 in profits, as this is your third year selling t-shirts and you have a good estimate of how much money you can earn at the concert. You arranged for a t-shirt supplier to provide customized t-shirts before the concert, but the supplier fails to supply them in time. He explains, "I was so overbooked, and your order simply did not get manufactured in time. Sorry."

Had you paid in advance for the t-shirts, it is probably clear you can seek a refund. But it does not fix the situation. You were relying on the $25,000 profit from selling t-shirts at the concert. When you explain your predicament to the supplier, it is likely he will push back on cutting you a check for the money to cover lost profits. Rather, the supplier will review the contract to locate any language relating to "lost profits." Perhaps, the supplier included in the limitation of liability clause that he would not be responsible for consequential damages. In that case, the supplier may be quick to claim such bars recovery of lost profits.

However, even if the supplier included this language, you could still argue lost profits under the circumstances were not consequential damages and are recoverable. Lost profits can arguably be treated as general damages. You may claim the supplier was fully aware the customized t-shirts were for a particular concert event and you were directly damaged by losing your expected profits. In other words, you can argue that the parties did not intend for lost profits to be consequential damages that cannot be recouped. In fact, the essence of the agreement was for you to resell the t-shirts at the concert and make a profit.

So where does this leave the parties and what is the point? Well, it leaves the parties with an unexpected surprise after the breach and a dispute that may be costly to resolve. The takeaway is that when negotiating a business contract, you should be sure to determine whether lost profits can be recoverable in the event of a breach. If you are the t-shirt supplier, you can specifically preclude recovery of lost profits. In effect, you may want to explicitly provide that you will not be responsible for the lost profits of the buyer, no matter what occurs.

However, if you are the buyer, you may want to cross out such language and, perhaps, even specify that "lost profits" are included as direct damages and owed should the t-shirts not be delivered in time. Alternatively, the buyer may desire to negotiate a liquidated damages clause that covers him for the lost profits upon breach. That way, the parties have a clear formula for the amount due should the supplier fail to perform under the agreement.

The Point:

- Regardless of which side of the deal you are on, put thought into whether "lost profits" are recoverable under the contract. The issue can get murky when a breach occurs.

- It is not safe to assume that lost profits are automatically included in a consequential damages waiver set forth in a limitation of liability clause, as the other party may think otherwise.

- It is better to be clear about the parties' intentions upfront and not overlook the issue of whether lost profits can be recouped following a breach. If parties can explicitly set forth their intentions on this issue in the agreement, they may be able to avoid uncertainty and costly disputes later on.

7.   **Avoiding Juries**

Leaving a business dispute in the hands of a jury can be risky. If the parties do not expressly waive a jury trial in the business contract, they can be faced with an unpredictable, time consuming and costly dispute should litigation commence. Generally speaking, parties to a commercial dispute may prefer that a judge, instead of a jury, resolves all disputes arising from the contract. To accomplish this, it is common for parties to express the intention of giving up their right to a jury trial by inserting, often in caps, the following language (the latter being more comprehensive).

> *EACH PARTY IRREVOCABLY WAIVES TRIAL BY JURY IN ANY ACTION OR PROCEEDING WITH RESPECT TO THIS AGREEMENT.*

OR

> *EACH PARTY IRREVOCABLY WAIVES, TO THE FULLEST EXTENT PERMITTED BY LAW, ANY RIGHT TO TRIAL BY JURY OF ANY CLAIM, DEMAND, ACTION, OR CAUSE OF ACTION ARISING UNDER OR RELATING TO THIS AGREEMENT OR ANY OF THE TRANSACTIONS RELATED HERETO, IN EACH CASE WHETHER NOW EXISTING OR HEREAFTER ARISING, AND WHETHER IN CONTRACT, TORT, EQUITY, OR OTHERWISE.*

Jury waivers, like the above, are extremely common in business contracts. Without this language, parties can be rolling the dice with a group of peers who can be less experienced and unpredictable in deciding commercial disputes.

The Point:

- Having contract disputes handled by a judge, instead of a jury, can provide greater predictability, less costs and expediency.

- If parties agree to have disputes heard by a judge, be sure to include language to expressly waive a trial by jury in the business contract.

8. Unwanted Publication of the Parties' Relationship

When parties decide to work together, they should consider what each of the parties can announce to the public about the business relationship. You may welcome the publicity and encourage the other party to disclose publicly that the parties are doing business together. However, more commonly in commercial arrangements, one party or both parties desire to be more discrete. A party may not want the other party to embellish the relationship or put out press releases touting the business partnership without prior approval. For this reason, parties who wish to exercise control over any public messages that are released about the parties' business relationship will want to include a clause on media releases. A typical media provision looks like this:

> *Neither Party will issue any press releases, make any other disclosures regarding this Agreement or its terms or use the other Party's trademarks, trade names, logos or other proprietary marks without the other Party's prior written consent, which consent shall be in such Party's sole discretion.*

If you do not discuss this subject with your counterparty and include language to fit the parties' expectations, you may be surprised to find a press release you did not approve publicizing the business relationship.

Furthermore, public communications and marketing can be accomplished on many different media platforms. In other words, if you are concerned about announcements on Twitter, you can add language saying so. Given the modern world of the Internet, parties may desire to be more specific on marketing limitations if they so choose. By way of example, parties can agree:

Each Party shall seek the prior written consent of the other Party before publishing the other Party's name and/or logo as a business partner of the other Party in any blog posts, Twitter posts, Facebook status updates and any other publicity or marketing materials.

Without such language, you may not be consulted in the publicity of the parties' business relationship.

The Point:

- Be sure to discuss in advance whether the parties desire to publicly announce their business relationship or prefer no publicity.

- If you want to have control over public announcements, make sure to require the counterparty to obtain your written consent prior to issuing any press releases, making public comments, or posting on social media.

9. The Unexpected Surprise of Prejudgment Interest

Separate and apart from interest owed on late payments discussed in the chapter on Payment Terms, is prejudgment interest a party can collect if a dispute proceeds to court and final judgment. Prejudgment interest is often overlooked by the parties and comes as an unexpected surprise when the court orders a party to pay a substantial interest payment on the judgment amount.

What most fail to recognize is that interest can accrue on the amount of a legal award from the time of breach, the date performance was due, or the time between the filing of a claim and when final judgment is entered by the court. The period of time for litigation to run its course can be long. Like years. And interest rates can be higher than expected, with each state having separate laws setting statutory prejudgment interest rates and accrual dates. New York's statutory interest rate is as high as 9% per annum, with other states even higher. What a great return on investment!

Practically speaking, though a party may have been deprived of money owed while it waited for the court to rule, prejudgment interest can make a party better than whole. Think of it this way: If you are the non-breaching party, you may be making more money with prejudgment interest than you could potentially investing money in bonds or in the stock market. The wait you endured to get paid while the parties duked it out in litigation does not seem so bad when you are entitled to recover interest payments at such high rates. Thus, while a non-breaching party may feel like it takes an eternity for the court to issue a judgment, that delay may be lucrative, as the party is racking up interest charges to collect should it succeed in winning the case. Feels good to be the prevailing party in litigation.

At the same time, if you are the party who may lose the case, you will want to inquire about the applicable statutory prejudgment interest rate and your potential exposure. Often times, parties do not realize they could be subject to paying prejudgment interest and fail to consider this when moving forward with litigation. You may be thinking twice about litigating to judgment once you inquire about the other party's right to recover prejudgment interest, which can add up. At a minimum, you want to explore any options available to stop the clock on prejudgment interest.

The Point:

- Parties often overlook that the prevailing party in litigation can not only win money damages, but can also recover prejudgment interest at favorable rates, which, while not intended, could mean a windfall for that party.

- If you are the breaching party, factor in prejudgment interest when evaluating your exposure, and before you go the distance in court. This amount alone could make an early settlement seem like a bargain.

10. Be Mindful of Over-Lawyering

Commercial terms will often be negotiated by the business team, but when it comes to putting the agreed terms on paper, lawyers are brought into the contracting process. Once the attorneys take over, a variety of different scenarios can transpire.

Managing Your Legal Counsel—What to Expect

The following is by no means meant to encompass every different scenario that can occur when an attorney takes over the contracting process. (That would bore you to death.) Rather, it is meant to highlight how to have a productive relationship with an attorney when negotiating and drafting a business contract.

Scenario One: The Good

You may be fortunate and work with an efficient attorney who is accustomed to reviewing and commenting on agreements and can negotiate a business contract to closure in a short period of time. The attorney may have commercial sense and the ability to understand when to push for certain terms and when to compromise and seek resolution. In such a case, the attorney may act as a business partner and engage in problem solving to accomplish the company's commercial goals. The attorney may also draft terms that are clear and concise. If this is all done without delays or unnecessary legal fees, good for you for picking this attorney!

Scenario Two: The Bad

You may, on the other hand, work with an attorney that views the contract process as a game, a win-lose situation. While the attorney may genuinely believe he or she is trying to get the best bargain for you as the client, the attorney can lose sight of the commercial objectives. The attorney may go crazy marking up the agreement. Before you know it, you have spent days, even weeks, going back and forth redlining a standard business contract. Perhaps the attorney does not fully comprehend that sometimes "done is better than perfect." Or worse, the attorney says "no" too often to the other side and jeopardizes the business relationship with the other party.

If you do not establish ground rules, you could be left with a large legal bill. Many parties have witnessed expensive hourly fees escalate because of trivial tasks, like fixing commas in an agreement. You may also be stuck explaining to the business that the benefits of the partnership are now delayed until the next quarter, as negotiations continue to be dragged out by lawyers.

With that said, sometimes prolonged contract negotiations can be worthwhile. There are certainly occasions when you need a tough negotiator and hammering out a deal takes time. For example, if you have a significant business venture, like a merger and acquisition or a complex commercial partnership, by all means aim for perfection. But, such is not typically the case in every day practice. Negotiating a business contract does not always require the Cadillac of legal work. There are also circumstances when you may be wasting time (and money) pontificating with your attorney over potential exposures in a commercial relationship that are not practical or real. Rather, they are some hypothetical, rare event unlikely to occur. Be mindful of when this happens, and decide whether it is worth it to continue down that path.

Some attorneys may disagree and argue it is important to cover all of your bases and negotiate every point in an agreement. However, parties have to recognize there is a line where legal can overtake the business objectives. As such, they should be mindful of "over-lawyering". For example, a company can hire an expensive law firm that charges thousands of dollars to mark up a simple four-page contract agreement or a cookie-cutter non-disclosure agreement. By the time the agreement is executed, the business has lost the revenue that could have commenced earlier, the hourly bill becomes a shocker when the invoice is received, and the contract sits in a desk (or on the cloud) to collect dust, never to be seen again.

Furthermore, should a dispute arise down the road, parties are often incentivized to work out a resolution. In most cases, ultimately, no matter what the contract says, the business may value the relationship with the other party and seek a business solution, not a legal or litigious one. That is the reality. If the parties want to continue working together, they are likely not going to involve lawyers when a dispute arises. Unless the stakes are high, limit the use of threatening legal action, involving lawyers and filing public lawsuits. Rather, make every effort to resolve the conflict with your counterparty, offering business compromises and preserving the commercial relationship. Fighting over contract disputes can become expensive (lawyers are not cheap), time-consuming, and unpleasant.

The Point:

- Understand ahead of time what you really need from an attorney when seeking to paper a business contract. Set expectations to limit the back-and-forth so you are not dragging out lawyer time.

- Contract negotiations do not always have to be complicated or long-drawn out processes.

- While you may strive for perfection in drafting a contract, never lose sight of the commercial objectives and the fact that most contract disputes are resolved between parties amicably to preserve the business relationship.

CHAPTER 6

The NDA Explained

At the beginning of a relationship, you may decide to provide confidential information to the other party for the purpose of exploring whether to work together. You may not be sure whether to pursue a business relationship with the other party yet. If that is the case, before you hand over confidential information, consider executing, at the outset, a document called a "non-disclosure agreement," which is commonly referred to as an "NDA" or Confidentiality Agreement.

An NDA contains clauses that provide for the non-disclosure and non-use of confidential information. It is a promise by one party to the other to protect confidential and proprietary information. In other words, it is one party telling the other: "Before I share any confidential information, you must agree to protect my secrets." After an NDA is executed, and once you have decided to move forward with the relationship, you can incorporate confidentiality terms in the commercial contract itself (as discussed earlier in the book in the section on confidentiality provisions). You can also, alternatively, reference and incorporate into the contract the NDA executed between the parties.

"Unilateral" vs. "Mutual" NDAs

There are essentially two types of commonly used NDAs: (1) a unilateral or one-way NDA and (2) a mutual, bilateral, or two-way NDA. The "unilateral" NDA is a confidentiality agreement that only addresses one party providing confidential information to the other party. Only one party is disclosing information and the other party is obligated to maintain its confidentiality. All of the provisions in the agreement relate to one of the parties disclosing confidential or proprietary information to the other party and the protections that surround such disclosure. In effect, the "unilateral" NDA is designed to be one-sided.

By contrast, a "mutual" NDA is entered into when both parties in the business relationship will be providing information to each other and they desire certain protections over each of their disclosures. Each party is obligated to keep the other's non-public information confidential.

The main difference between a "unilateral" NDA and a "mutual" NDA really just boils down to which parties are protected when providing confidential information. If an NDA states that both parties are providing confidential information and uses the parties' names in generic terms, such as "Receiving Party" and "Disclosing Party," with paragraphs beginning with "Either Party" or the "Parties," it is probably a mutual NDA Agreement. If an NDA only uses one party's name as the discloser of information, then it is a unilateral agreement.

Stated simply, before you exchange confidential information about your business, think about whether you are protected and consider asking the party to sign an NDA prior to disclosing information. If both parties are providing confidential information, enter into a "mutual" NDA; if only one party is providing confidential information, a "unilateral" NDA makes more sense.

In practice, however, a party may nonetheless insist on executing a mutual NDA, even if it does not plan to produce confidential documents. Mutual NDAs can be more balanced, as they are drafted with both parties' interests in mind. Also, should circumstances change and the initial non-disclosing party ends up providing confidential information, that party is already protected under a mutual NDA. No need to execute a second NDA, yet another legal document with more time and money spent. Believe me, you will be questioned why a mutual NDA was not simply used in the first place. Moreover, always be sure to read a mutual NDA to confirm it really is mutual and does not have provisions that favor one party over another (unless the parties deliberately agree to an imbalance).

Having said that, to the extent you prefer never to receive confidential information from the other party, say so, and keep to a unilateral NDA. While the other party may request a mutual form, if you really do not want to be receiving confidential information, or do not want to be restricted from using any information received, make that clear and stick to a unilateral NDA, preferably using your own template.

Confidentiality Terms: What to Expect

Generally speaking, all NDAs follow a similar routine, cookie-cutter format. They typically begin by containing a definition of the term "Confidential Information." This definition is intended to describe what exactly the parties consider to be confidential information. You will likely come across a confidentiality provision that contains a broad definition, which considers a number of categories or types of information to be considered confidential information and thereby protected under the agreement. Sometimes a disclosing party will put together a laundry list of information, documents, and technology that it could dream of that may be disclosed to the other party and it considers confidential. For example, a broad definition of confidential information looks like this:

> *"Confidential Information" shall mean any information disclosed by either Party to the other Party, either directly or indirectly, in writing, orally, electronically, or other media format, including (but not limited to), business records and plans, invention summaries, inventions, technical information, patent, patent applications, customer data, customer lists, customer names, designs, algorithms, financial analysis, financial information, forecasts, formulas, hardware configuration information, know-how, ideas, discoveries, market information, marketing plans, processes, products, product plans, research, specifications, software, source code, trade secrets or any other information which is designated as "confidential," "proprietary" (or could otherwise be reasonably construed as confidential under the circumstances surrounding disclosure), or any third-party information that the Disclosing Party has an obligation of confidentiality to protect. Information disclosed orally as confidential by the Disclosing Party shall be considered Confidential Information.*

If you are reviewing a confidentiality provision like the above, assume the other party wants to preserve the argument that pretty much anything it provides can be considered confidential information. The key language to locate in a provision like this is the following line, *"or could otherwise be reasonably construed as confidential under the circumstances surrounding disclosure."* Such language is inserted as a catchall to encompass any information a reasonable person would consider confidential under the circumstances.

If you are the one providing information, you are likely going to ask for this language. This is for the simple reason that a party does not want to have to fit every type of information it provides in some sort of category listed above to be considered confidential information. Rather, a party wants this catchall language to provide added protection in case it discloses something that does not fall neatly into one of the categories expressly listed as confidential information. The disclosing party often wants to preserve the argument that any and all information disclosed to the other party is potentially covered under the NDA as confidential information. In other words, the disclosing party typically insists on casting the widest possible net for the confidential treatment of its materials.

But what if you are the receiver of information and are uncomfortable to agree to such broad language? You may not be interested in agreeing to confidentiality restrictions that state everything you receive is claimed to be confidential information, thereby limiting your use of it in the future. No need to fret. There are a few common practices in these circumstances to limit such broad language.

First, you can cross out the categories listed above that you believe are too broad or inapplicable under the circumstances. In effect, you can narrow the scope of the definition of confidential information. For example, you may decide the categories of "ideas" and "discoveries" are too vague and encompassing. Also, consider the type of information that may be disclosed. You may prefer agreeing to a shorter list of types of information that actually have commercial value and reflect trade secrets.

Moreover, you can also cross out the language *"or could otherwise be reasonably construed as confidential under the circumstances surrounding disclosure."* Then, replace it with language that requires your counterparty to physically mark or label the information it asserts as confidential on the materials provided. That way, it is cleaner and there is no confusion over what information is considered confidential information under the agreement. Such language looks like this:

> *"Confidential Information" shall mean any information disclosed by either Party to the other Party which (a) if in writing, is conspicuously marked "Confidential", "Proprietary" or other similar marking on the materials at the time of disclosure, or (b) if provided orally or visually, is identified as confidential at the time of disclosure and confirmed in writing to recipient within 10 days of such disclosure.*

With that said, however, practically speaking, you may get push back on this type of language. Such language can be helpful or impractical, depending on the circumstances. In practice, the disclosing party may not want to worry about labeling each document it believes to be confidential with the words "Confidential." The disclosing party may be concerned that any documents that are not marked as such would be considered by you to be fair game. Moreover, stamping each document as "Confidential" can be time consuming and burdensome. The disclosing party may find this to be a hassle. Given this, consider what type of documents, as well as the volume of documentation, you are sharing to determine whether identifying them as confidential is actually logistically reasonable under the circumstances.

If it is not really feasible to be marking all material handed over with a "Confidential" label, expect the disclosing party to say "no thank you" to this change. However, if you are not sharing volumes of information, you may insist on a cleaner process where confidential documents are marked as such so you know what you can or cannot use.

Exclusions from Confidential Information

Another practice you can consider, and also a key provision in an NDA, when dealing with a broad definition of confidential information is to get comfortable with the exclusions of what does *not* constitute confidential information. Certain information cannot reasonably be expected to be treated as confidential. Thus, in nearly all confidentiality agreements, parties discuss certain exclusions that will *not* be considered confidential information. If you do not see such exclusion language like the below, you will want to add it, as it is typical and standard for all NDAs.

For simplicity sake, exclusions essentially protect the receiving party who may be thinking: "Hey, not everything you claim is confidential information needs to be treated as such. We need rules here about what cannot be considered secretive or protected information subject to this NDA." To that point, parties set forth categories of information that should *not* be treated as confidential because it is not so secretive. These categories are routine, are set forth in every NDA, and encompass the below topics. You may have noticed that these categories are exactly the same as discussed in the prior chapter of this book dealing with confidentiality provisions in a business contract.

Publicly Available Information. Information that was publicly known, whether before the information was disclosed, or after the information was disclosed if it was through no fault of the receiving party, is not considered confidential information. In other words, if information was or becomes generally known, and not because the receiving party disclosed the information, then it is not included as confidential information.

Information Already Known to Receiving Party. Information already known to and in the possession of the receiving party prior to the receipt from the disclosing party is not considered confidential information. You may also see language that requires the receiving party to show, through its books and records, that the information was already known to it prior to disclosure. That way, the party cannot just fabricate that it had the information prior to disclosure, but rather is required to show actual evidence of its independent prior possession.

Third-Party Source. If the information was obtained from a third party, and that third party was free of any obligation of confidentiality (*i.e.*, that third party is not breaching an NDA or other confidentiality restrictions), the information is not to be considered Confidential Information. The recipient has to rightfully receive the information from a third party.

Independently Developed by Receiving Party. If the information was independently developed by the receiving party without use of the confidential information or breach of the NDA, it would not be considered confidential information. You may also see language that requires the receiving party to show, through its books and records, that the information was independently developed by the receiving party. The disclosing party may seek to review actual evidence to verify such was the case.

Written Permission by Disclosing Party. Information that was specifically approved in writing by the disclosing party for the receiving party to release would not be considered confidential information. In effect, the disclosing party gave the receiving party permission, in writing, to disclose the information.

The exclusion language looks like this:

Confidential Information shall <u>not</u> include any information that:

i. *was publicly known and made generally available in the public domain prior to the time of disclosure by the Disclosing Party;*

ii. *becomes publicly known and made generally available after disclosure by the Disclosing Party to the Receiving Party through no action or inaction of the Receiving Party;*

iii. *is already in the possession of the Receiving Party at the time of disclosure by the Disclosing Party;*

iv. *becomes available to the Receiving Party on a non-confidential basis from a source not bound by confidentiality restrictions that cover the relevant information;*

v. *is independently developed by the Receiving Party without use of or reference to the Disclosing Party's Confidential Information; or*

vi. *Disclosing Party gave written permission to Receiving Party to disclose.*

Practically speaking, if you receive information that your counterparty claims to be confidential and use this information to your benefit or disclose this information to a third party, you will want to fall under one of those categories, should your counterparty claim foul. It could play out, for example, that your counterparty complains you disclosed certain information to a third party and argues you breached the agreement. You may respond by asserting that one of the exclusion categories applies, such as the information was already online and is publicly available (but, of course, not because you posted it online).

The good news is that most NDAs have similar exclusion language, like the above, and you don't have to spend much time crafting your own exclusions. Attorneys have, for the most part, thought through different scenarios whereby it does not make sense for confidential information to be treated as protected information. You may see some variations to the above categories, and you should question and understand such variations, but the exclusions in NDAs are mostly routine and will look similar to the above.

The Point:

- Regardless of whether you are the recipient or discloser of non-public information, read carefully the definition of confidential information set forth in an NDA and decide whether it is too broad or too narrow under the circumstances.

- The party receiving confidential information should consider whether labeling documents as "Confidential" can be practically implemented or will be too cumbersome for the discloser.

- Both parties should carefully review the exclusions to the definition of confidential information to make sure they encompass the standard exclusions and that they are comfortable with the rules of the road.

Other Parts of an NDA

Non-Disclosure

Non-disclosure language sets forth how the receiving party shall maintain the confidentiality of the disclosing party's confidential information. It literally says, "Do not disclose my information to others who do not need to know this information." The disclosing party wants to make sure confidential information will be kept in strict confidence and will not be communicated to any third party without permission. Typically, you will also see language regarding the standard of care a party expects you to maintain for confidential information. Something like this:

The Receiving Party shall maintain the confidentiality of the Disclosing Party's Confidential Information and will not disclose such Confidential Information to any third parties. Such efforts shall consist of at least the same degree of care exercised by the Receiving Party with respect to its own confidential information of a similar nature and in any event shall be no less than a reasonable standard of care.

The above language is standard and basically relays that the receiving party should treat the disclosing party's information as if it were its own. It also provides that the disclosing party expects, at a minimum, for the receiving party to handle information as a reasonable person would under the circumstances. Essentially, the non-disclosure language is about who is permitted to view the confidential information and the standard of care required to maintain the confidentiality of the information.

If you come across a standard of care requiring "best efforts," be aware that this can be interpreted as the highest and most onerous of the standards of care. This language can be understood as: "Everything that can be done should be done to protect the confidentiality of the information." It can seem excessive. Unless the disclosing party is handing over extremely sensitive or top-secret confidential information (like *Coca-Cola's* recipe), a receiver of information will want to consider deleting that language and maintaining a more common "reasonable" degree of care.

The non-disclosure language may also provide further limitations on the disclosure of the confidential information. For example, it can prescribe who you can share the information with, explaining that certain officers, directors, employees and advisors can receive the information on a need-to-know basis. It is also typical to insert language that requires the receiving party to advise each recipient of the restrictions in the agreement prior to disclosing any of the confidential information. Further, it is commonplace for the NDA to require the receiving party to notify the disclosing party immediately should it become aware of an unauthorized disclosure (or any other violation of the agreement), as well as cooperate in good faith to rectify the matter.

In addition, if a party wants to keep the business relationship itself private, an NDA may contain language to that effect. The NDA may state that the receiving party will not disclose to anybody that confidential information has been made available, that the parties are discussing a transaction, or any other information with respect to the parties' negotiations or status thereof. In other words, the fact that the parties executed an NDA itself will be considered confidential. Such restriction may make sense if the parties have legitimate reasons for their preliminary talks to remain secretive. Practically speaking, if this type of language is in the NDA, make sure those that know about the parties' discussions, and not just those that receive the confidential information, are told about this restriction. It is one thing to glance over and agree to this language in an NDA, but it is another thing to make sure you, and others in your business, are actually complying.

Limitation of Use

While non-disclosure language says do not disclose to others, the limitation of use provision says how the receiving party can use the information. It is standard to have a provision upfront in the agreement that states the intended "purpose" for which the information is provided. For example, the purpose could be to explore a particular business transaction or to engage in discussions about a joint venture or, more generally, business endeavors. Whatever the purpose, it will often be followed with language providing that the receiving party will only use the confidential information for a stated purpose. This "purpose" language is standard in an NDA to ensure the receiving party does not go off and use confidential information for whatever it pleases. The last thing you want is the receiving party stealing proprietary information and using it to make money.

Ownership of Confidential Information

The disclosing party flexes its muscles in the ownership section of an NDA and makes clear that any confidential information disclosed is owned by such party. The disclosing party is letting you know it is not conveying any legal rights to you over this information. The language is designed to remind you that the disclosing party has protected legal rights (such as intellectual property rights) and it is not handing over any of these rights through the disclosure of the information. For example, you may see language like:

> *This Agreement does not convey to the Receiving Party any ownership interests in any of the Disclosing Party's*

intellectual property rights. No rights or licenses to trademarks, copyrights, patents or other intellectual property or proprietary rights are implied or granted under this Agreement.

This kind of language is routine for a disclosing party to include in an NDA. The disclosing party may be providing the receiving party proprietary information. As such, the party wants to make crystal clear in the NDA that it is the exclusive owner of this information and the receiving party is not entitled to any legal rights over it. In other words: "In case there is any confusion, any intellectual property disclosed is not yours, it is mine." Different language, while rare, might seek to transfer intellectual property rights from the disclosing party to the receiving party. If you are the disclosing party, you probably want to remove it. Fast.

No Warranty or Representation

Entering into an NDA typically happens early in the business relationship. At that point, you are doing the dance of sharing information to decide whether to work together. Given that the parties are not yet agreeing to form a business relationship, you will often see language in an NDA making clear that the disclosing party is not promising the receiving party anything with respect to the information shared. The language often states the disclosing party is not warranting or promising the receiver that the confidential information is accurate or complete. The disclosing party is typically saying to the receiver: "My information says what it says and I am not claiming it is entirely truthful, or that you can rely on this information as being accurate or complete."

Think of it as a similar situation to purchasing a used car off Craigslist. The seller may tell you that you can take the car as you see it on the driveway and the seller wants no responsibility if something goes wrong. As with the car example, an NDA typically provides that the receiving party takes the information "as is." And, if the receiving party chooses to rely on such information, it does so at its own risk.

The language in a mutual NDA looks something like this:

No Warranty. The Receiving Party accepts all Confidential Information of the Disclosing Party on "as-is" basis, and acknowledges that, with regard to such Confidential Information and any other information provided to the Receiving Party pursuant to this Agreement: (i) the Disclosing Party shall not have any liability as a result of the use of, or reliance on, any such information; and (ii) the Disclosing Party has not made and will not make any representation or warranty as to the accuracy or completeness of such information.

At first glance this may sound unfair. But the reality is that it is too early for a discloser of confidential information to promise anything to the receiving party. If you are disclosing information during the NDA phase, you are just providing the other party information so you both can decide whether to enter into a business relationship. It is still the courting stage. Should the parties continue negotiations and commit to terms, expect a separate agreement apart from the NDA to cover any representations and warranties. In other words, during the initial phases, before any agreement is reached on a business deal or money is exchanged, it is standard for an NDA to limit exposures and liabilities by not offering any guarantees over information provided. Once the parties decide to move forward, promises and assurances can be made in the business contract itself.

Government Requests/Subpoenas

NDAs also include provisions to deal with a situation where a third party uses the legal process to seek disclosure of confidential information from the receiving party. Indeed, now that you possess proprietary information, it is possible that a third party may use legal means to request you turn it over. For example, a government agency, such as the Securities and Exchange Commission, can request disclosure of confidential information in your possession. Also, the receiving party may be brought into a litigation, such as when a party seeks documents (or what is known in the legal world as "discovery") from third parties, for example.

In legal terms, you can receive a document that is called a third-party "subpoena." This is a legal document that requests the receiving party to turn over certain categories of documents, which could include confidential information received pursuant to an NDA. To account for such circumstances, NDAs typically contain standard language that require the receiving party to provide the disclosing party with prompt notice about any subpoenas it receives regarding the protected information. The clause also provides that the receiving party will cooperate with the disclosing party so the disclosing party can pursue measures to maintain confidentiality of the information or seek some other forms of protection. Such language typically looks like this:

> *If a subpoena concerning any Confidential Information is served on a Receiving Party or the Receiving Party becomes legally compelled (by oral questions, interrogatories, request for information or documents, civil investigative demand or any other legal process), to disclose any of the Confidential Information, the Receiving Party shall, if permitted by law, notify in writing the Disclosing Party promptly upon receipt of the subpoena or other legal process. The Receiving Party shall cooperate with any lawful effort by the Disclosing Party to contest the validity of the subpoena,*

to seek a protective order, or to pursue other legal process to protect the Confidential Information.

The premise of this standard language is to allow the disclosing party the opportunity to seek confidential treatment of the information sought by a third party or the government, and other applicable protections, prior to disclosure. In practice, if you have a good relationship with the disclosing party, you probably want to notify that party should you received a subpoena requesting its information. That would be the professional thing to do, regardless of whether it is explicitly written in the NDA. The only exception to this would be a unique situation that prohibits you from telling the other party about an investigation.

Additionally, often NDAs contain language that the receiving party may make disclosures of confidential information to the extent required by law (*e.g.*, by court order or other legal or administrative directive). The NDA may, however, restrict such disclosure to only *"that portion of the confidential information which, based on the reasonable advice of counsel, is legally required to be disclosed."* Although this can seem boilerplate, in practice such language can require the receiving party to obtain the advice of legal counsel—which effectively means spending money to retain outside counsel. It also can put the receiving party in a bind if it is unclear what is legally required to be disclosed under the law. This can lead to a situation where the receiving party is forced to obtain a legal opinion on whether information can remain private or needs to be disclosed, resulting in larger fees. If you are concerned about this language and do not want to spend money on legal fees if a third party seeks to obtain confidential information from you, consider adding that any legal fees expended will be *"at the Disclosing Party's sole expense."*

Return or Destroy

NDAs put obligations on the receiving party to return confidential information and/or destroy all copies at the end of the NDA. An NDA may also require the receiving party to certify in writing that it has complied with the provision to return or destroy. While this is standard language, in practice it is common for a party to archive one copy of the information in case disputes arise in the future, if it is required by law, or should the information be difficult to retrieve and destroy. Moreover, with cloud-based storage and other forms of data archiving, it can be difficult to fully destroy or return all confidential information. The clause looks like this:

> *Receiving Party shall, upon termination of this Agreement, or upon written request of Disclosing Party, whichever is earlier, immediately return or destroy at Disclosing Party's option all copies of such Disclosing Party's Confidential Information and certify in writing its compliance with this requirement, except that Receiving Party may retain a copy of such Confidential Information solely for archival purpose or to the extent deletion is prohibited by applicable law.*

The above language is standard, but as a receiver of information, you may not want an automatic requirement to return or destroy the confidential information at a future date. You could forget to do so. In practice, the receiving party does not always actually return all of the information to the disclosing party. Parties often agree to this language but don't necessarily enforce it. Nevertheless, if you don't think you are going to follow through with this obligation, consider modifying the above language such that the disclosing party must request information be returned or disclosed before you are required to do so legally.

Remedy: Injunctions

The remedy provision in an NDA addresses the forms of relief a party may seek to obtain in the event of a breach of the NDA. Think about what happens when you are the disclosing party and you learn that the receiving party disregarded the NDA and is revealing your secrets (or threatens to do so). For example, you find out the receiving party is disclosing your confidential information to a third party, perhaps a competitor, in violation of the NDA. In such a case, you may want to run into court and seek to stop the disclosure. To make this an easier process, most NDAs have language that expressly allows a party to seek a court order stopping the unauthorized disclosure of confidential information. This type of remedy is called an "injunction" in the legal world.

Thus, language in an NDA seeking "injunctive relief" or what is also referred to as "equitable relief," allows the disclosing party to rush into court to prevent continued wrongful disclosure. Asking for injunctive relief in an NDA is common, since the primary goal of an NDA is to keep information secret. Injunctive relief is a mechanism to block disclosure of such information.

The provision looks like this:

Each Party acknowledges that any disclosure, use or misappropriation of Confidential Information of another Party in violation of this Agreement would cause such Party irreparable harm for which there may be no adequate remedy at law. Accordingly, each Party agrees that such other Party shall have the right to apply to any court of competent jurisdiction for injunctive relief, without prejudice to any additional remedies available to it at law or in equity.

The above clause is meant to clearly provide that a disclosing party has the option to seek injunctive relief (a court-order to stop disclosing secrets). It also makes clear that the disclosing party can seek other remedies available. Specifically, the language specifies that injunctive relief is "without prejudice to any remedies available to it at law or in equity." This means the injured party can seek injunctive relief or potentially pursue other available remedies, such as monetary damages. Allowing a party to seek any remedies in "law or in equity" pretty much encompasses everything available a party can seek to obtain relief.

If you are the disclosing party, be aware of alternative language in an NDA that seeks to make the injunctive remedy your "only" available form of relief. In other words, look out for language in a remedy provision that states injunctive relief is the "sole" or "only" form of relief a disclosing party can obtain. A disclosing party may prefer to pursue additional forms of relief should the receiver breach the NDA. For example, a disclosing party may desire financial compensation if it suffered losses. Thus, it probably does not want to limit its relief to "solely" or "only" injunctive relief.

Thus, a disclosing party should keep an eye out for any language limiting the forms of relief it can seek if the NDA is breached by the other party. This principle of being aware when the counterparty inserts a "sole" remedy phrase is equally applicable to terms in business contracts. Should a party designate a particular remedy as the only remedy, the other party wants to read the provision carefully. This type of language could restrict such party from recovering its full losses during a breach, which may not be desirable.

Finally, it is important to be mindful whether you are disclosing more information than necessary after you sign an NDA. No need to give away the crown jewels unless you have a strong commercial justification. While an NDA can be drafted airtight, in reality, the other party can disregard the NDA and still pass along your sensitive commercial information. Therefore, be smart about what you disclose.

What to Watch Out for in an NDA

Non-Solicitation Clause

Some companies like to include a clause in an NDA that prohibits the other party from soliciting and hiring its employees. The clause may have language preventing the other party for as long as three years from hiring the other party's employees. The clause will look something like this:

> *Party A agrees that for a period of three (3) years from the date of this Agreement, Party A shall not (and will ensure that no person or entity under direct or indirect control of Party A), solicit, entice or employ any of the officers, directors or employees of Party B, or its subsidiaries or divisions.*

In most cases, a non-solicitation clause is inappropriate to include in an NDA. Think of it this way: Do you want to explain to Human Resources or your boss that you entered into an NDA with a company, shared a few confidential documents, and now for three years cannot hire anyone from that company? Doubtful. For this reason, one suggestion is to search for the word "solicit" or "hire" in an NDA to make sure to locate any non-solicitation clause. Then cross it out. Remember, when negotiating an NDA, parties are often in the early exploratory phase of exchanging information and have yet to agree to even work together. Generally speaking, it may not be reasonable at this preliminary stage to bind a party to a commitment not to hire any of the counterparty's employees.

This is not to say it is never appropriate to agree to a non-solicitation clause in an NDA. In certain situations, such as when

NDAs are signed prior to negotiating major transactions, it can make sense. For example, you may come across a non-solicitation clause in an NDA when parties are discussing the sale of all or part of a company. The seller could be worried that a potential buyer may induce employees to work for that potential buyer. Should the transaction not develop, the seller could be left with no deal and now also fewer employees. To avoid such occurrence, a seller may insist on including a non-solicitation clause in the NDA.

Should you feel obligated to agree to a non-solicitation clause, consider whether to make it mutual, so you too are protected. You can also negotiate a shorter non-solicitation period and limit the non-solicitation to employees who were participants of the contemplated transaction. Furthermore, you can add language that allows you to employ individuals who approached you about a job without your encouragement, whether by responding to a job post or reaching out through a recruiter. Such language looks like this:

> Each Party agrees that for a period of twelve (12) months from the date of this Agreement, a Party shall not (and will ensure that no person or entity under direct or indirect control of such Party), solicit, entice or employ any of the officers, directors or employees of the other Party, or its subsidiaries or divisions, having been involved in this contemplated transaction. The prohibition contained in this clause shall not apply to the recruitment of any employee who has answered a bona fide public advertisement or been recruited by an employment agency and the Party employing the employee has not given (directly or indirectly) any form of encouragement to the employee to do so, or advised such employment agency to approach the employee.

With that said, it is important to reiterate that in an ordinary business contract, you want to push back when the other party includes a non-solicitation clause. If you are not careful, a non-solicitation clause can come back to bite you, especially if the NDA is with a potential competitor. At a minimum, require a convincing justification before agreeing to a non-solicitation restriction.

Unusually Long Terms

Most NDAs have language providing how long confidential restrictions need to remain in place. An NDA should generally contain an expiration date. Typically, an NDA provides that confidentiality obligations will last for two to five years from either the date the agreement is executed or from the date materials are disclosed. Such a provision will look like this:

> *Your obligations hereunder shall expire three (3) years from the date of execution of this Agreement.*

While anywhere between two to five years is typical, if you come across an agreement that has a longer time period, perhaps even in perpetuity, inquire with the other party about the need for such an extended restriction period. The reality is that information becomes stale, the value of information diminishes over time, and parties need an ending period to stop worrying about preserving confidentiality. Moreover, it can be expensive and administratively burdensome to maintain the secrecy of information for an unreasonably long term. Thus, if you are receiving confidential information, consider negotiating a shorter time period.

Having said that, depending on the information exchanged, the disclosing party may want to resist an end date and restrict the information for as long as possible. The disclosing party could be thinking: "After the expiration date, the receiving party may believe it is free to use or disclose the confidential information. Am I going to find this information, three years later, online in a public forum or on the front page of a newspaper?" In real life, the answer is probably no. Nonetheless, if a party is disclosing super secretive information (such as trade secrets) and needs to maintain confidentiality without time limitations, it can make sense to agree to language stating just that, like the following:

> The Agreement shall remain in effect with regard to Confidential Information that qualifies as a trade secret under applicable law, for as long as such information continues to qualify as a trade secret.

Signature Requirement

You may occasionally come across language in the non-disclosure section that requires a receiving party to have any employee or third party who views confidential information to physically sign an NDA or acknowledge through a signed agreement that it has read the NDA. Depending on the circumstances, it may not be practical to have every employee that comes in contact with the counterparty's information sign a separate agreement. If you see language stating that you need to get signed agreements from all those involved, consider whether you will actually do such a thing. If not, do not agree to it. The alternative is to agree to inform those who receive confidential information of the NDA and the confidential nature of the information, rather than make them physically sign a separate agreement. Instead of requiring a signature from each employee who has access to the information, you can include the following language:

> The Receiving Party agrees that it will limit the dissemination of the Confidential Information of the Disclosing Party within its own organization to such individuals whose duties justify their need to know such information, and then only provided that there is an understanding by such individuals of their need to

maintain the confidential and proprietary nature of such information and to restrict its uses to the purposes specified herein.

Indemnification Clause

In certain circumstances, an NDA may contain an indemnification clause, which was discussed earlier in this book. With respect to an NDA, a disclosing party may seek to have the receiving party indemnify it for claims, liabilities, costs and expenses (including reasonable attorney's fees) if the receiving party breaches the agreement. Basically, the indemnification requires the receiving party to pay for any claims arising from its unauthorized disclosure of confidential information.

Often the receiving party will not agree to an indemnification provision in an NDA. An indemnity for breach of an NDA is not as common and typically resisted as it will potentially increase the liability of the receiving party. A receiving party may not want the added exposure of allowing the disclosing party to recover for all claims, liabilities, costs, and expenses incurred in connection with a breach. Instead, the receiving party would rather just be on the hook for damages actually and directly suffered by the disclosing party as a result of the breach. While in most cases an indemnification provision will be inappropriate in an NDA, there will be times when such is still requested. A disclosing party may have specific business reasons for seeking added protections. However, practically speaking, few recipients would be willing to give an indemnity in favor of the discloser for breach of an NDA.

Working with Competitors

There may be times when you are contemplating a business relationship or a transaction with a competitor. Use extra care scrutinizing an NDA in these instances. For example, an NDA could include language that prevents a receiving party from using confidential information to compete with the disclosing party. If parties are not competitors, this type of language could make sense and may be agreeable. But, if parties are already in a competitive relationship, or could potentially be competitors in the future, you may not want to agree to such language. This is what such a provision can look like:

Receiving Party undertakes, in particular, that the Confidential Information, which you acknowledge may be of commercial value to you, shall not be used by you, your representatives or by others through or under your direct or indirect control in developing like or competitive business enterprises or ventures or to the competitive disadvantage or detriment whatsoever of the Disclosing Party.

If you read this provision in an NDA and you are, or may be in the future, in a competitive relationship with the other party, cross it out. Further, you may decide to explain to the other party that the companies can be construed as having competitive business models and therefore cannot agree to such a restrictive provision.

On the other hand, if you are concerned about entering into an NDA with a competitor, consider adding language to affirmatively protect yourself against any confusion, such as the below:

In no event shall either Party be precluded from discussing, reviewing, developing for itself, having developed, or developing for third parties, materials competitive with the Confidential Information, irrespective of their similarity to the Confidential Information, so long as such Party complies with the terms of this Agreement.

OR

This Agreement shall not preclude or limit the independent development by or on behalf of any Party of any products or systems involving technology or information of a similar nature to that disclosed hereunder or which compete with products or systems contemplated by such information, provided that it is done without use of or reliance upon the other Party's Confidential Information.

Over Lawyering

Finally, you should look out for over lawyering when it comes to plain vanilla NDAs. Some attorneys have a tendency to drag out negotiations of an NDA, quibbling over minor points. While you may want to strive for perfection when negotiating an NDA, you should not lose sight of the reality that NDAs have a certain cookie-cutter feel and may not receive much attention after being signed. Indeed, over lawyering an NDA can leave a bad taste in the other party's mouth, as it can often be the first glimpse of how the parties do business together.

Additionally, in reality, enforcing an NDA requires hiring an attorney and filing a lawsuit. This will be unpleasant, expensive, potentially public if it lands in the courts, and will likely damper (perhaps even ruin) the business relationship with the other party. Nobody wants to be dragged into court for a dispute over an NDA. Thus, when spending time and legal resources doing the NDA dance, consider the key terms discussed herein and implement practical safeguards, such as limiting the information disclosed and the number of recipients, to protect against a leak.

Moreover, it is worth pointing out that an NDA is not the only means to protect against the misuse of secretive information. States have laws against the misuse of trade secrets by theft, bribery or fraud and you can, if necessary, sue under trade secret laws for misappropriation. So, there are other legal means besides the NDA to protect business secrets.

In short, when you are reviewing an NDA, keep these realities in mind and negotiate points that matter, such as that your trade secrets, proprietary technology and sensitive financial data stay secret. Just don't sweat the small stuff.

The Point:

- NDAs have become standardized to include basic clauses that spell out such topics as: what constitutes confidential information (and what does not), who can and cannot receive information, how information should be kept secret and for how long, who owns the information, and what to do if a third party seeks to obtain confidential information.

- Also commonplace are provisions addressing whether the disclosing party is disclaiming the accuracy of the confidential information, how to return or destroy such information when the relationship is over, and what relief the disclosing party can seek if confidential information is leaked.

- Beware of clauses that are hardly standard, including those that attempt to prevent a receiving party from soliciting or hiring the disclosing party's employees, or restricting competition between parties, potentially for years.

- While NDAs are important to protect the secrecy of confidential information and allow a party to safely share such information, so too is the business need to explore commercial relationships without unnecessary delays and over lawyering of plain vanilla NDAs.

CHAPTER 7

Last Words

We all have, at some point in time, entered into a business contract without really understanding what was written on the paper. Although the same basic terms are widely used in nearly all business contracts, they are commonly misunderstood and often times unnecessarily convoluted. Let's face it, many smart, reasonable people have no idea why certain legal-sounding clauses are inserted into a contract and do not have sufficient resources to fully grasp what they mean. Chances are we do not learn of our mistakes until something goes wrong. By then, it can be too late.

The purpose of this book is to provide you with contracting tools and a comprehensive roadmap so you can understand a business contract from start to finish. The goal is simple. Take everyday contract terms and make them easy to understand. The book was written to be a practical guide, to have commercial sense, and to be realistic. It is time to evolve, so the contracting process is more accessible and relatable to the modern businessperson. There is no reason why both parties cannot know exactly what they are signing.

The Final Point:

- Anyone can understand what is written in a commercial agreement once they learn about the main terms found in almost all business contracts.